GLORY DAYS

East Kent

Glyn Kraemer-Johnson
and John Bishop

Ian Allan PUBLISHING

Front cover:
On a gloriously sunny day in the summer of 1965 Park Royal-bodied Guy Arab III FFN 390 stands outside Deal bus station, awaiting further passengers on local route 83 to Mill Hill. The presence of the Morris 1000 and, in the distance, a Morris Oxford and an Austin A40 Farina serves to remind us that the then British Motor Corporation once enjoyed a sizeable share of the British car market. *John Bishop*

Back cover:
Numerically the first of a batch of 12 delivered in 1948, Dennis Lancet CJG 988 was one of a number of similar vehicles to have their Park Royal bodywork converted in 1958/9 from rear- to forward-entrance layout and rebuilt with full front to facilitate pay-as-you-enter operation. Ready to depart for Martin on rural route 93, it is seen at Dover's Pencester Road bus station in the company of Park Royal-bodied Guy Arab IV MFN 903 with blinds set for service 61 to Margate. *John Bishop*

CONTENTS

Title page:
By June 1973, when this photograph was taken in Canterbury bus station, the effects of NBC livery policy were being felt, but AEC Regent V/ Park Royal PFN 874 remained defiant, albeit with NBC advertisement on the nearside. By comparison the livery of AFN 781B does not in the photographer's opinion bear comment. *John Bishop*

Below:
A fascinating picture of the East Kent garage at Rye, East Sussex, taken from the ancient town wall. Typical of medium-sized, functional buildings put up by operators (and very much ignored by photographers), the building still exists today, being occupied by a firm of timber merchants. However, it has long since ceased to resonate to the sound of Dennis Lancets, such as those seen here standing alongside. The left-hand Lancet coach is EFN 589, whilst the rebuilt Lancet is CFN 127; lurking inside the garage is an unidentified dual-purpose AEC Reliance. In the background is the River Rother, beside which once ran the Rye–Camber Tramway. *Charlie Turton*

First published 2005

ISBN 0 7110 3030 8

Published by Ian Allan Publishing

an imprint of Ian Allan Publishing Ltd, Hersham, Surrey KT12 4RG.

Printed in England by Ian Allan Printing Ltd, Hersham, Surrey KT12 4RG.

Code: 0504/B1

INTRODUCTION

How many bus operators can claim to have assisted in the evacuation of Dunkirk? Or that one of its vehicles co-starred with Brigitte Bardot? How many major companies operated Morris Commercial and Leyland TS1 double-deckers or managed perfectly well without the use of fleet numbers? All of these are claims that can be made by the East Kent Road Car Co Ltd, a BET subsidiary whose red-and-cream buses tootled quietly around the southeasternmost corner of our island, hardly attracting the attention of enthusiasts . . . or at least the enthusiast press. For so it would seem. Look on any bookstall at any rally and you'll find numerous publications on London Transport, Southdown, Ribble and Crosville. There will be books on municipalities and on independents both large and small, but you'll be exceedingly lucky to find anything on East Kent. In fact I'm surprised you found this one! Even magazine articles are few and far between.

Why this should be isn't easy to understand. Southdown's popularity is often said to be due to the fact that in their formative years many enthusiasts spent holidays in the company's area and that its buses are therefore evocative of happy times. Surely the same must apply to East Kent, whose area included the towns of Margate, Ramsgate and Herne Bay — resorts that in the 'Fifties and 'Sixties were every bit as popular as Brighton, Eastbourne and Worthing. Southdown's superb apple-green-and-primrose livery is also said to be a contributory factor to its popularity, but (in the authors' opinions, at least) the cherry red and ivory of East Kent is just as attractive. Like Southdown, East Kent eschewed the popular 'reversed' bus livery for its coaches with cream as the predominant colour; instead it painted them in the same rich dark red as its buses. In fact, in prewar days, its coaches were painted in two subtly different shades of red, and magnificent they looked too. On the bus side, Southdown's full-fronted PD3s were unique, apart from a few one-offs and rebodies on older chassis, and have acquired cult status. East Kent's full-fronted AEC Regent Vs, on the other hand, have faded into oblivion, even though, apart from Liverpool Corporation, few other operators took similar buses.

So what accounts for our interest? John's roots are in the region, his grandparents having lived in Dover and Herne Bay, and his interest was kindled on visits to the area. As for me, I was born on the wrong side of the Medway and came to the Company relatively late in its life. My interest stemmed from a love of Guy double-deckers and the rich red-and-cream colour scheme, the combination of the two on the 'MFN' Arab IVs resulting in what were just about the most beautiful things ever to run on four wheels.

Whatever the reason for the neglect of East Kent, we hope this book will go some way towards redressing the balance. The authors have taken the 'Glory Days' as being from 1928, when the first new double-deckers arrived, to the early 1970s, by which time the Company had become part of the National Bus Company and the poppy-red livery was beginning to make its presence felt. The book is not intended to be a concise history of East Kent, nor is it a technical volume; rather, it is a nostalgic and light-hearted look in words and pictures at the vehicles, services and events in the life of a company that holds a special place in the hearts of both authors. Whereas most of the major operators were known as 'Motor Services' or 'Omnibus Company', East Kent shared with Lincolnshire and West Yorkshire the rather Tilling-esque title of 'Road Car Company', which immediately gave the impression that it was something a little different — as indeed it

▲ An undated view, believed recorded at Canterbury, depicting at least two identifiable East Kent vehicles in beautifully lined-out livery. The first, bound for Deal, is an ex-British Automobile Traction, Macclesfield, Daimler CD (M 5575), acquired in 1918 and sold in 1928. The long-lived fleetname had already been adopted. The second, waiting to depart for Whitstable, is a Tilling-Stevens TS3 (FN 3693) with an open-top body, new in 1919 and later rebodied with Short Bros bodywork before being withdrawn in 1932. The glory days were already in the making. *Arthur Ingram / Glyn Kraemer-Johnson collection*

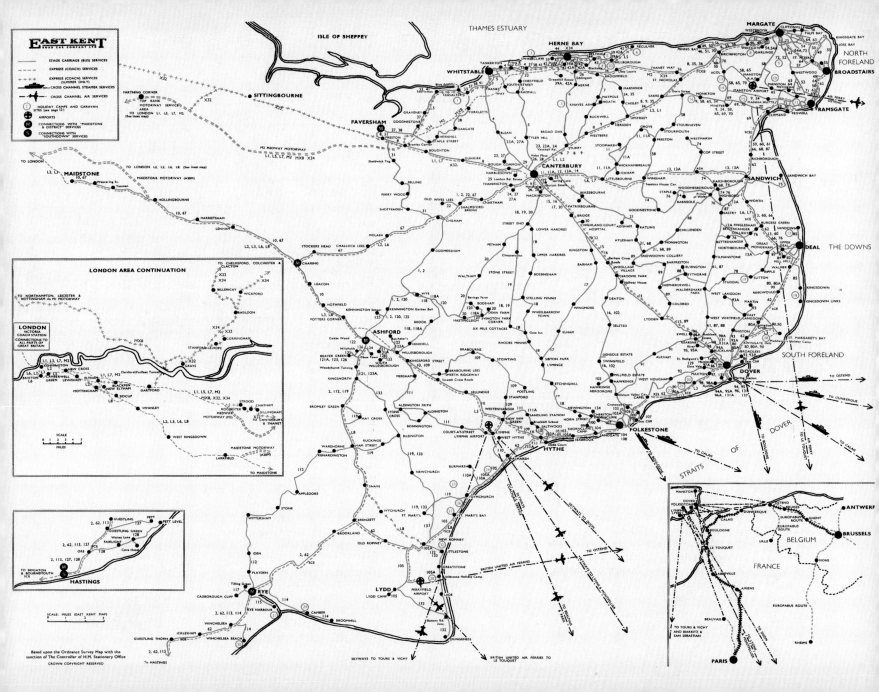

was. Space has not permitted a picture of every type, nor is every vehicle or modification mentioned in the text. For those looking for this level of detail we recommend the excellent *Illustrated Fleet History of East Kent 1916-1978* published by the M&D and East Kent Bus Club, now unfortunately out of print but available from some public libraries.

As far as the early history of East Kent is concerned, suffice it to say that the Company was formed in 1916 with registered offices in Canterbury. Sidney Garcke, son of Emile Garcke, founder of the British Electric Traction (BET) group, was appointed Chairman, whilst the Board included Walter Flexman French, who had been very much involved in the formation of both Southdown and Maidstone & District, which could be described as sister companies and, indeed, always seemed that way. However, unlike the territory served by the other two, the population of eastern Kent was centred very much on its towns, large areas such as Romney Marsh being very sparsely occupied. Because of this and engineering difficulties such as expensive tunnelling, the development of the railways in this southeastern corner was also sparse. Thus, in the 'Twenties, when the holiday trade began to grow, it was largely the bus that was called upon to handle the extra custom. Stage-carriage services were developed to handle the holiday traffic, and a wide range of excursions into the Kent countryside was introduced.

The Company's geographical location was to play an important part in its history, in a variety of ways. Even during World War 1 lighting restrictions on the coast meant that passengers were instructed not to tender paper money after dark, because conductors had difficulty in distinguishing values. Shortage of petrol also meant that some buses were converted to run on coal gas, the gas being carried in bags mounted on the vehicles' roofs. The high winds experienced on the coastal roads made use of these bags difficult, and on one especially windy day the bags on two buses were ripped from their mountings and carried out to sea. Their eventual destination is not recorded, but, assuming they crossed the Channel, the Germans must have thought the British had invented some new kind of airship!

Shorncliffe Barracks, at Cheriton, near Folkestone, became the base for troops preparing to leave for France, and the 'Red Buses', as they had become known, were frequently filled to overflowing by soldiers anxious for a 'final fling' before embarkation — so much so that military personnel had to be employed at Cheriton to supervise loading and, on alighting, the collection of fares. As the war progressed wounded soldiers were returned to Folkestone Harbour and buses were frequently commandeered to transport them to the Royal Pavilion Hotel, which was in use as an emergency hospital. Buses were also required to transport thousands of Belgian refugees shipped to Folkestone following the advance of the German army.

Although a few new services were started during World War 1 it was not really until hostilities had ceased that expansion began in earnest. The rail strike of 1919 brought about the introduction of the first express services to London, another operation which was to grow during the following years. As was the case with most of the major companies, East Kent's expansion during the 'Twenties came largely through the acquisition of smaller operators, more than 50 being taken over.

Following the Great War the fleet had been badly in need of renewal, and replacements came mainly in the shape of Tilling-Stevens TS3 and Dennis Y-type chassis with bodies by Short Bros of Rochester, Brush, Tilling or East Kent itself. All were single-deckers. In fact it was not until 1927 that the Company introduced its first double-deckers. These were three new Daimler Y-type chassis (FN 8092-4) on which were mounted open-top Straker bodies bought from the London General Omnibus Co, which had in turn inherited them from an acquired independent. Following experiments with these buses it was decided to place an order for the Company's first double-deckers and, with the single-deck fleet modernised, the 'Glory Days' had begun.

Glyn Kraemer-Johnson
Hailsham, East Sussex
November 2004

Bibliography

East Kent Road Car Co Ltd, Illustrated Fleet History 1916-1978,
(M&D and East Kent Bus Club, 1978)

A History of East Kent Road Car Company Ltd by Frank Woodworth,
(Capital Transport, 1991)

ABC East Kent Buses & Coaches by S. L. Poole (Ian Allan, 1949)

◄◄ Map of East Kent routes *c*1965.

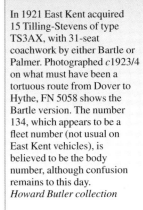

▲ In 1921 East Kent acquired 15 Tilling-Stevens of type TS3AX, with 31-seat coachwork by either Bartle or Palmer. Photographed *c*1923/4 on what must have been a tortuous route from Dover to Hythe, FN 5058 shows the Bartle version. The number 134, which appears to be a fleet number (not usual on East Kent vehicles), is believed to be the body number, although confusion remains to this day.
Howard Butler collection

5

1. MAINLY OF TITANS AND IMPERIALS
Prewar double-deckers

In the late 1920s Leyland Motors launched a new range comprising Titan TD1 double-deck chassis and the Tiger TS1 single-decker, still at this time with petrol engines. Somewhat perversely East Kent purchased four Tiger TS1 chassis and had them bodied (by Short Bros) as open-top double-deckers! Although motion makes identification difficult this vehicle, seen on the seafront at Margate, is believed to be FN 9095. When delivered these buses lacked destination blinds, this feature being added later in the 1930s. In 1945 this vehicle was rebodied as a single-decker.
J. T. Wilson / Southdown Enthusiasts' Club

The three open-toppers proved successful in operation, and it was decided that double-deckers should be tried on a wider scale. An order was therefore placed for four Leyland Tiger TS1 single-deck chassis! However, this was not quite as crazy as it sounds, for they were fitted with open-top double-deck bodies by Short Bros of Rochester. Quite why the single-deck chassis was chosen when the double-deck Titan TD1 was available isn't clear, although some rather unkind critics suggested that the Company wanted to make the transition from single- to double-deck in easy stages. Delivered in July and August 1928, they were registered FN 9093-6. Whatever the reason for its choice, the combination obviously worked well, for another, similar vehicle (FN 9544) was delivered in 1929 and was followed by a further five (JG 651-5) in 1930.

The subsequent history of the TS1s is interesting. By the outbreak of World War 2, although most were still fairly sound mechanically, their open-top, open-staircase bodies were outdated and not really acceptable. Two of the original batch were withdrawn from passenger service, but even these weren't wasted: FN 9096 had its body scrapped after it was damaged by enemy action in 1940 and in its place was given a lorry body that had formerly graced a Daimler CD type; FN 9093 was withdrawn in 1944 and subsequently converted to a tree-lopper. FN 9544, the solitary 1929 example, was requisitioned by the Admiralty and never seen again, but the remaining TS1s were all rebodied. FN 9094 and JG 652 received new utility double-deck bodies by Park Royal in 1942, but FN 9095 and JG 651/3-5 were all given 34-seat single-deck bodies by Burlingham in 1945, thus — after some 15 years' service — finally assuming the role intended for them by their chassis manufacturer!

It is probably appropriate at this point to explain East Kent's fleet-numbering system — or rather the lack of one! Although photographic evidence exists of vehicles carrying numbers, there is some suggestion that these in fact referred to paint dates. Whatever their purpose, no fleet-numbering system was in general use until the advent of the National Bus Company and the introduction of computerised records, *i.e.* outside the scope of this book. Until then identification of vehicles was by registration number, and this was achieved by reserving registrations in advance and ensuring that numbers were not duplicated, although batches of similar vehicles were not numbered consecutively. For instance, the postwar Guy Arabs were registered EFN 170-209, FFN 360-99, GFN 908-937 and MFN 883-901. However, only one bus at any one time would carry any given number, so, providing the fleet didn't exceed 999, the system worked well. In fact it makes one wonder why so many concerns, particularly municipals, bothered carefully matching fleet and registration numbers, when the registration number alone would have sufficed!

Back to East Kent's prewar double-deckers. In 1930 the first 'true' double-deckers appeared, in the shape of six Leyland TD1s delivered between June and November. They were registered JG 977/8, 1057/8 and 1411/2 and carried Leyland's own 51-seat lowbridge bodywork. They were a vast improvement over the Short-bodied TS1s, having covered tops and enclosed staircases although the lowbridge design was something of an awkward necessity. The lowbridge layout had been developed by Leyland itself and featured a sunken gangway on the offside of the upper deck which protruded into the lower saloon and was the cause of many a bump to forgetful passengers who stood up in a hurry! The offside gangway necessitated four-abreast seating

In 1930 East Kent took delivery of further Leyland products in the form of the double-deck Titan TD1 chassis and the Tiger TS1 single-decker. However, as if to prove its earlier point, the Company had a number of TS1s fitted with open-top double-deck bodies by Short Bros (although these would be rebodied later in life as single-deckers). One such, JG 655, is seen in Thanet whilst on layover between journeys on route 2. Note the smart white-capped East Kent crew sitting towards the rear of the lower saloon.
J. T. Wilson / Southdown Enthusiasts' Club

The Leyland Titan TD1 heralded the 1930s with a quantum leap in bus design. Enclosed stairs, roof, pneumatic tyres and reliable mechanics all spelt success for the bus industry and the death-knell to some of the small branch railway lines. Illustrating the type's distinctive piano-style front, JG 977, seen at Faversham on the long route to Margate via Canterbury, shows how much faith was put in these vehicles when delivered in 1930. This example was to serve the Company for 15 years.
The Omnibus Society

In 1931 East Kent took delivery of another four lowbridge all-Leyland Titan TD1s, of which JG 1623 is seen during World War 2 on hire to Venture, of Basingstoke, Hampshire. Note the white edging around the wings and guardrail on the side. The state of the offside front tyre reminds one that such items were in short supply.
The Omnibus Society

Although today associated mainly with Dover, passenger traffic to France was once shared with Folkestone. The hilly nature of the latter town meant that large engineering works, including the viaduct in the background, were necessary for the rail network to reach the harbour and Dover. The sparkling 20-seat bus, JG 1477, is a Beadle-bodied Morris Commercial Viceroy dating from 1931. The gas lamp on the street corner, boys wearing caps and the motorcycle chugging along behind the bus complete this early-1930s scene.
The M&D and East Kent Bus Club

upstairs, making access difficult both for passengers and for conductors trying to collect fares. However, the design reduced the vehicle's overall height by around 12in and thus made it possible for double-deckers to be used on routes where low bridges precluded the use of a normal-height vehicle. In the 'Thirties, therefore, the side-gangwayed double-decker proved the answer to providing extra capacity on services with height restrictions, and all new double-deckers purchased by East Kent during the decade were of this type.

The Leyland TD1 with lowbridge Leyland body appeared to have become the standard double-decker, four more (JG 1621-4) arriving in 1931, but appearances can be deceptive, and few would have forecast the 1932 deliveries.

Morris Commercial chassis had for some time been chosen for the single-deck and coach fleets, but it was still a surprise when East Kent became one of only two operators to order the newly introduced Imperial double-deck chassis (the other being Edinburgh Corporation). This was no 'toe-in-the-water' exercise, for no fewer than 15 were ordered for delivery in 1932, followed immediately by an order for a further 10 which arrived at the turn of the year. The Imperial and its

single-deck counterpart — the Dictator or RP type, of which East Kent also had a number — were designed by Charles K. Edwards, who had previously been Chief Designer with AEC. A feature common to both types was a facility for the engine, gearbox and radiator to be easily disconnected and 'wheeled' from the vehicle for maintenance purposes. Whilst the choice of chassis was unusual, to say the least, the Imperials received lowbridge 55-seat bodies by Park Royal, thus commencing a relationship with a coachbuilder which, apart from a few hiccups, would be the major bodywork supplier until the NBC imposed its own purchasing policies in the 'Seventies.

The first 15 Imperials, which arrived in the summer of 1932, were registered JG 2601-15, the second batch becoming JG 2906-15. In May 1933 a further four — JG 3227-30 — were received, bringing the total of such vehicles to 29. A 30th Imperial was HA 7639, an ex-demonstrator with a Short Bros body that had appeared at the London Motor Show in 1931. The Imperial remained in production for only two years, and so no further orders were placed by East Kent. Indeed, the type had a very short life with the Company, all being withdrawn by 1939. All were scrapped with the exception of JG 3229, the chassis of which was fitted with a

tanker body, in which form it survived with the Company
until 1943.

Some three years would elapse before the next delivery of
double-deckers, and these showed a return to the tried and tested
Leyland chassis. Twenty TD4s — JG 7010-29 —arrived in the
spring of 1936 and were the Company's first oil-engined double-
deckers. Originally intended to be of type TD4c, with torque
converters, they were delivered with normal gearboxes. They
carried 55-seat lowbridge bodywork by Brush, of a design not
dissimilar to that fitted by Park Royal to the Imperials. However,
whereas the destination display on both the TD1s and Morris
Commercials had consisted of a single-line ultimate destination
only, the Brush bodies had a protruding front indicator box that
featured an additional small square aperture to the nearside of
the destination; although intended to display a route number, this
box was sometimes used to show a (very cramped) 'via' point.

A further order called for no fewer than 50 TD4s, this time
with 53-seat Park Royal bodies. Again, these were similar to
those fitted to the Imperials, but the front upper-deck windows
were shallower, considerably changing the frontal appearance.
The destination display, meanwhile, was altered further, the
main box being enlarged to show the ultimate destination and
up to three lines of intermediate points — a layout that was to
remain standard for many years. Delivered during the winter of
1936/7, these buses were registered JG 8201-50.

Until this time the companies taken over by East Kent had
been small, with only a few vehicles (and sometimes only one),
invariably single-deck. In 1937, however, two comparatively
major undertakings were acquired. One involved no vehicles
at all, this being the Dover Corporation Tramways system.
Discussions had been taking place for some years, and it was
eventually agreed that on 1 January 1937 the trams would be
abandoned, their place being taken by East Kent buses. Under
the terms of this agreement receipts from Dover-area services
were to be pooled and 75% of any surplus paid to the Corporation,
protective fares that had been in force to safeguard the tramways
being abandoned. As already mentioned, no vehicles were
involved in the takeover, the trams all being scrapped. The tram
depot was leased to East Kent and, although not used immediately,
would come into its own in 1942, when the Company's main
Dover garage suffered bomb damage.

The services acquired from the Corporation filled an important
gap in East Kent's growing empire. So too did those of the
Thanet tramways — or, to give it its full title, the Isle of Thanet
Electric Supply Co (IoTESCo) — which undertaking operated
both trams and buses in the Margate, Ramsgate, Broadstairs and
Westgate areas. Again, discussions had been taking place for
some time about the abandonment of the trams and the possible

sale of the undertaking, which was proving unprofitable, even with its motor buses. Agreement was eventually reached, and the undertaking was sold to East Kent in August 1936. From October of that year the network was operated by East Kent on an agency basis pending the withdrawal of the trams, the abandonment finally taking place on 25 March 1937.

The Thanet trams were replaced by new Leyland TD4 double-deckers, but the 49-strong IoTESCo motor-bus fleet passed to East Kent in its entirety, and, although some were operated for only a few weeks, others were repainted into East Kent livery and remained in the fleet for several years. Amongst the acquisitions were a number of double-deckers. Apart from two Thornycrofts with Vickers open-top bodies (KP 418/9), which were never operated by East Kent, all were of Daimler manufacture, IoTESCo having standardised on this type since 1929. Two CF6s with open-top bodies (KR 5085/6) were disposed of almost immediately, whilst FS 3388 and KV 103, both former Daimler demonstrators with lowbridge bodies, lasted little more than a year. Stars of the double-deck fleet, however, having been new earlier in 1936, were five Daimler COG5s, with 56-seat highbridge bodies — the first of this layout to enter the East Kent fleet — by Weymann. The COG5 chassis featured a pre-selective gearbox coupled to a Gardner 5LW engine — a power unit that was to become very familiar with the Company's engineers in the years ahead. They were registered ADU 47 (this being another ex-demonstrator) and CKP 876-9. All five received East Kent livery and would remain in the fleet until 1950.

The beginning of 1938 saw more Leylands, this time to the upgraded TD5 design. Twelve (JG 9907-18) had lowbridge bodywork by Park Royal, whilst 13 were bodied by Brush to the same layout (JG 9919-31). The turn of the year saw the arrival of a further 40 TD5s. All fitted with the now familiar 53-seat lowbridge bodywork by Park Royal, these were the first vehicles in the fleet to carry three-letter registrations (AJG 1-40).

As it happened, the TD5s would be the last prewar 'deckers delivered to the Company. Ten Leyland TD7s, again with lowbridge Park Royal bodywork, were ordered but, although they received Canterbury registrations (BFN 932-41), were diverted to Crosville Motor Services of Chester, to which company they were delivered in July 1940 and with which they remained until withdrawal in 1957.

The glory days of the East Kent Road Car Co began during the Leyland, Guy and Dennis era, when such chassis were graced with handsome Park Royal bodywork. In this scene, recorded at the workshops in the late 1930s, highly skilled staff are applying the finishing touches to five immaculate Leyland Titan TD4s with lowbridge Park Royal bodies. Identifiable are JG 8220, dating from 1936, and JG 8235 and (possibly) JG 8229, dating from 1937. Flat caps and short-back-and-sides haircuts were the order of the day. *The M&D and East Kent Bus Club*

Seen in Ramsgate, with the harbour in the background, JG 8226 was one of a batch of 50 Leyland Titan TD4s delivered in 1936/7, their Park Royal bodywork being fitted from new with full-size destination and route-number boxes. Is the lady with the pram staring in wonderment at the new bus or longing for the return of the Thanet trams? *The Omnibus Society*

2. CROUCHING TIGER, LEAPING EXPRESS
Prewar single-deckers and coaches

FN 9023, Tilling-Stevens B10C2 delivered in 1928, was converted into a lorry upon withdrawal. Scrutiny of the bodywork reveals it to be an old bus body. Records show that the vehicle was converted *c*1937, being finally withdrawn in 1949 and scrapped in January 1951. *The Omnibus Society*

During the 1920s single-deckers purchased by the Company had been mainly of Daimler, Tilling-Stevens and Morris manufacture. However, as was the case with most operators at this time, the acquisition of smaller concerns had brought into the fleet a myriad of chassis types, including such exotic marques as Lancia, Gilford and Fiat, although many remained for only a short time. However, some semblance of standardisation began to appear from 1928, when the first Tilling-Stevens Express B10s were delivered.

Contrasting with the petrol-electric TS series previously favoured by East Kent, the B10 was a conventional chassis with a 40hp four-cylinder petrol engine. The 1928 deliveries comprised 28 B10C2s, the order for bodywork being shared between three coachbuilders. Six (FN 9001-6) were fitted with 37-seat bodywork by Beadle of Dartford, 19 (FN 9007-25) received similar bodies by Brush, whilst the final three (FN 9541-3) were given 32-seat coach bodies by Short Bros. All had rear entrances — an arrangement favoured for the majority of full-size single-deckers and coaches until the advent of the underfloor engine. The Beadle bodies lasted only until 1933, when they were replaced by 32-seat Park Royal coach bodies, and in the following year FN 9007-11 were similarly treated.

No fewer than 52 B10s were delivered in 1929. Of these 43 had 37-seat bus bodies by Brush (FN 9906-30) or Short Bros (FN 9931-48), the remaining nine (FN 9901-5/49/50, JG 298/9) having coach bodies by Short Bros. Of these, FN 9949/50 were particularly interesting in being of normal-control layout (*i.e.* with the driver behind the engine), being intended for 'long tours' and 'special' private-hire work.

It was in 1929 that joint working with Maidstone & District was established. The service in question was between Folkestone and Maidstone, a distance of 36 miles, and both companies used their latest Tilling-Stevens B10 single-deckers. The venture was so successful that another joint service, this time between Canterbury and Maidstone, was introduced the following year.

Of course, the routes to Maidstone were basically bus services, but East Kent had operated express coach services for some years. In fact the area's first express service, operating between Deal and London, had been introduced as early as 1914 by the British Automobile Traction Co, but unfortunately this ran for only a few months before the war intervened. However, by 1919, when a sudden rail strike in the South East left thousands of holidaymakers stranded, the recently formed East Kent company, along with a number of smaller operators, provided services from the Kent coastal resorts to London. The journey from Folkestone took some five hours, and the fare was £1 single, £1 10s (£1.50) return — quite a lot, when one considers the earnings of the time.

Throughout the 'Twenties competition was fierce and, as most of the traffic was during the busy holiday season, the winter months saw too many coaches chasing too few passengers. However, the 1930s witnessed a consolidation of the network, due not only to the acquisition of competing operators but also to the introduction of picking-up and setting-down points on the fringes of London in what would now be termed 'the commuter belt'.

Also established during the 'Twenties was what was to become the well-known 'South Coast Express' service. By 1928, when our story starts, East Kent was operating a service between Folkestone and Hastings, Maidstone & District and Southdown were working a joint service from Hastings to Eastbourne, with a connecting service to Brighton, while Southdown alone was operating a lengthy service from Brighton to Portsmouth. So territorial were these companies that this situation might well have continued had it not been for Elliott Bros of Bournemouth (later to become Royal Blue), which applied to run an express service from Bournemouth to Margate. This made East Kent, M&D and Southdown sit up and take notice, and an application by them to run a similar service was granted, although M&D soon dropped out of the arrangement.

With the introduction of the 1930 Road Traffic Act Elliott Bros seized the opportunity to challenge Southdown's right to operate into Bournemouth. However, the South Eastern Area Traffic Commissioner, within whose area the entire route from Margate to Bournemouth operated, obviously felt that the public would benefit by having one service, and as a result of his decision a pooling arrangement came into operation. Under this Royal Blue worked the section between Bournemouth and Portsmouth while Southdown and East Kent operated between Portsmouth and Margate.

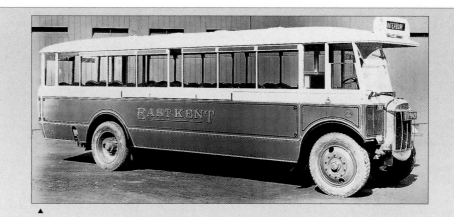

▲

In 1928 East Kent took delivery of 75 Tilling-Stevens B10C2 chassis bodied by either Beadle or Brush, these being followed later in the year by another three with Short Bros bodywork. FN 9012 was bodied by Brush, famous at that time for building tramcar bodies. Whilst looking very solid and splendid in the livery of East Kent, the body would be replaced after only five years' service. *Alan Lambert collection*

Compare this vehicle with Tilling-Stevens FN 9012 and it is hard to believe that the two are from the same batch. Close examination of the registration plate reveals that this is almost certainly FN 9004, rebodied by Park Royal in 1933. With updated treatment of the radiator and other refinements, members of this batch lasted until just after World War 2. *J. T. Wilson / Southdown Enthusiasts' Club*

▼

By the turn of the decade the Tilling-Stevens Express had become the standard for East Kent single-deck bus and coach chassis, and more were delivered in 1930. Also that year came a rather unusual purchase in the shape of 11 Gilford coaches acquired from Aldershot & District, to which company they had become surplus to requirements. Six had 20-seat bodywork by Strachan & Brown, and the remainder 24-seat bodies by Arnold & Comben. New in 1927/8, they would serve East Kent for about six years.

Whilst the Express chassis was proving ideal for the major services, many of the more rural routes needed something smaller. To meet this requirement the Company turned to Morris Commercial, a manufacturer it had patronised in the mid-'Twenties, when a number of 1-ton chassis had been fitted with 14-seat bodies built by East Kent itself. In 1931 it was the Morris Commercial Viceroy that was chosen, 34 being purchased. Sixteen (JG 1456-71) were fitted with 20-seat coach bodies by Thomas Harrington of Hove. Although this was a fairly local concern and one of the major suppliers to neighbouring Maidstone & District and Southdown, its products never featured very prominently in the East Kent fleet. By contrast another 'local' bodybuilder, J. C. Beadle of Dartford, was well

represented in all three fleets, and it was that firm which bodied the remaining Viceroy chassis (JG 1472-89), again with 20-seat bodies. The Harringtons were regarded as pure coaches and used as such, whereas the Beadles were used as buses during the winter months and as extra coaches when required.

Despite the popularity of the Tilling-Stevens and Morris Commercial, changes were afoot, five Leyland Tiger TS1 coaches with 32-seat Hoyal bodywork having been ordered for delivery in March 1931. In the event, these were delivered to Southdown, which was short of vehicles for the South Coast Express service. Registrations JG 1621-4/53 had been reserved for them, but they were re-registered by Southdown as UF 7856-60. They remained with Southdown for a year, eventually arriving with East Kent in March 1932, retaining their Brighton registrations. Thus, while East Kent's first Leyland TS1s had been double-deckers, their first new TS1 coaches were a year old when received!

Morris Commercial remained East Kent's favoured chassis manufacturer in 1932, when all new deliveries were of this make. As well as the Imperial double-deckers already described came 19 RP types, on which East Kent built its own 20-seat bodies, delivery stretching from October 1932 well into the summer of 1933. They were registered JG 2822-30/2-41, the missing JG 2831 having been diverted to the London & South Coast company. Further RPs (JG 3710-6) arrived later in 1933 with the now familiar East Kent 20-seat bodies. However, four more (JG 3717-20), delivered in early 1934, also with East Kent 20-seat bodies, were classified as coaches; these would be down-seated to 14 in 1937 and withdrawn the following year. Also received in 1934 were two more Viceroys (JG 4251/2), this time with Park Royal coach bodywork, which would turn out to be the last new Morris Commercials purchased by the Company.

In 1935 there arrived a new 'small bus' chassis — the first of a very long line of single-deck and coach chassis to be supplied by Dennis Bros of Guildford. The chassis in this case was the newly introduced Ace, a normal-control model that earned itself the nickname of 'Flying Pig' by virtue of its protruding bonnet; this in turn was a result of the front wheels being set back to provide a smaller turning-circle. It was a chassis which found popularity with a number of Tilling-group companies, and many were fitted with bodywork by the Eastern Counties Omnibus Co, later to become Eastern Coach Works; indeed, the first batch delivered to East Kent included 10 (JG 4241-50) with 20-seat bodies by

A superb study of Leyland Tiger TS7/Park Royal JG 5443 in 'as new' condition. The luggage area towards the rear of the roof is clearly visible, but note also the interior, complete with curtains and bright white cloth on the headrests. Externally, the vehicle has still to receive its sideboards.
The Omnibus Society

that concern. The remaining 16 (JG 4225-40) continued the tradition of having bodies built in the Company's own workshops, being not dissimilar to those built on Morris Commercial chassis; in fact these were the last bodies to be built by East Kent. All would be downgraded to bus work in 1936, replacing the earlier Morris Commercial 20-seaters. A further three Aces (JG 5449-51) were received in 1935, this time with well-appointed 20-seat coach bodies by Park Royal; used initially as back-up vehicles for the South Coast Express, they would be cascaded to bus work in 1940. The journey from Margate to Portsmouth on one of these little coaches can only be imagined!

The coach fleet was further expanded by more Park Royal-bodied Leyland TS7s, no fewer than 73 (JG 5420-48, 6501-36/93-600) being

The Dennis Ace was an ideal vehicle for lightly trafficked rural routes, thanks to its manœuvrability and ease of maintenance, and East Kent was soon taking full advantage of these attributes, 29 having been delivered in 1935. It is noteworthy that the Morris Commercial Viceroy and RP types purchased at the same time were withdrawn after very short lives, in 1938/9, whereas the Aces survived until well after the war. Eastern Counties-bodied JG 4248, with wartime-painted wings and guard rails, is seen on layover between journeys on Herne Bay local route 39 at Reculver, King Ethelbert, its driver apparently oblivious to the charms of the tearooms!
The Omnibus Society

East Kent's standard coach was the Leyland Tiger TS7 with Park Royal body, so heads must have turned in 1937 when the company acquired five Duple-bodied TS7s from MT Company (Motor Coaches) Ltd. One of these vehicles, CYL 243, is shown with the small fleetname, but note the even smaller version squeezed into the aperture above the destination display. Despite being non-standard, all five would serve the Company until 1954. *W. J. Haynes / Southdown Enthusiasts' Club*

Aside from the Aces and other acquisitions the first serious intake of Dennis products comprised a batch of 26 Lancets delivered in 1936 with Dennis bodywork similar in style to the contemporary Park Royal design. The first 20 had petrol engines, the rest oil, but within two years JG 6820, seen here *en route* to the Romney, Hythe & Dymchurch Light Railway station at Hythe, and its petrol-engined sisters would travel to Guildford to be fitted with diesel engines. *W. J. Haynes / Southdown Enthusiasts' Club*

Seen when Canterbury bus station was almost new in the 1950s is Leyland Tiger TS7 JG 6599. Dating from 1936, its chassis was originally fitted with the then standard 32-seat Park Royal coach body. However, in 1938 it received the body from JG 9944, which seated only 24 passengers, in a 2+1 layout, as its quiet and smooth-running petrol engine made it suitable for touring. Its cream roof and streamlined appearance made this very different from the rest of the coach fleet. *J. T. Wilson / Southdown Enthusiasts' Club*

delivered in 1935/6. By 1937 the chassis had been upgraded to the TS8, and 36 of these (JG 8979, 9932-66) joined the fleet in 1937/8, all but one having the familiar 32-seat coach body by Park Royal. The odd one out (JG 9944), intended for touring work, had a 24-seat forward-entrance body to a more curvaceous design, incorporating glass cant panels on the roof, and featuring 2+1 seating; this luxurious body was later exchanged with that on JG 6599, it being felt that the more refined running of a petrol-engined chassis would suit it better.

May 1937 saw the takeover of MT Motor Coaches of New Cross, London SE14, which brought into the fleet five Leyland TS7 coaches, three of which were just a year old, the other two being delivered new to East Kent. Although they had bodywork by Duple, with forward (rather than rear) entrances, they were sufficiently close to the Company's standard

specification to be painted in East Kent livery and retained in the fleet until 1954. Apart from their different but still handsome body design, they were easily distinguishable by their London registration marks, CYL 243-5 and DXV 740/1.

On the bus front, 1936 had witnessed the debut of a new type of full-size single-deck chassis, the Dennis Lancet, which was to remain the Company's standard single-decker until the early 'Fifties. Twenty-six (JG 6800-24, 7808) were delivered between February and July, all with 35-seat bus bodywork by Dennis itself. The first 23 were delivered with petrol engines (but would be fitted with Dennis oil engines in 1938); JG 6823/4 had the trusty Gardner 5LW diesel, while 7808 had a Dennis oil engine from new, these last three being actually classified as Lancet IIs. A further 24 (JG 8702-25), again with Dennis bodywork, arrived in the following year and were followed at the end of

Coaching excellence at London's Victoria Coach Station in the 1930s. Two East Kent Leyland Tiger TS7s with 32-seat Park Royal coachwork — JG 5431 and JG 6527 — combine with two Maidstone & District Tigers — CKO 964 and CKE 433 — to produce a classic line-up; Leyland really did appear to rule the coachways of England. Unfortunately JG 5431 would be badly damaged in 1940 and rebodied, although its original body was subsequently repaired and fitted to another of the same batch. *W. J. Haynes / Southdown Enthusiasts' Club*

Another view of 1935 Tiger JG 5431, here approaching journey's end in London and this time with later Park Royal body, with raised roof for the carriage of band instruments. Note that this body still has the same sweep of cream above the windows, thereby blending as far as possible with the rest of the fleet. The presence of the Green Line RF dates this view to the early/mid-1950s, JG 5431 being withdrawn after the holiday season in 1956. *Glyn Kraemer-Johnson collection*

the year by a solitary example with 35-seat Park Royal body (JG 9906), which bus had been exhibited at the 1937 Commercial Motor Show.

A further 19 Lancets entered service in 1939, five (AJG 41-5) with Park Royal bodywork and 14 (AJG 46-59) with the more usual Dennis. The Park Royal examples were rather odd in appearance, having full-length roof luggage racks designed for the carriage of musical instruments — a requirement dictated by the number of contracts gained by East Kent for the transport of military bands, most notable being the Royal Marines School of Music at Deal; this feature would also be incorporated on two of the 1935 Leyland TS7 coaches (JG 5431/3), rebodied by Park Royal in 1941, still as 32-seat coaches.

Six 20-seaters received in 1939 introduced another chassis make for the small bus, these being Leyland Cubs AJG 607-11 and BFN 176. The Cub had been introduced in 1932 and was Leyland's equivalent of the Dennis Ace, being of normal-control layout (though without the protruding bonnet) and capable of taking 20-seat bodywork. It had proved very popular with Southdown and with London Transport but was perhaps rather an odd choice for East Kent. Moreover, all five were fitted with second-hand bodywork: AJG 607-11 received East Kent bodies dating from 1933/4 and transferred from Morris Commercial RPs, whilst BFN 176 was given the Eastern Counties body from a withdrawn Dennis Ace.

By 1939 the Company could boast a fine fleet of modern, luxurious and decidedly handsome coaches and a single-deck bus fleet that had developed from the myriad types of the 'Twenties into a fleet of largely modern and fairly standardised vehicles. This, then, was the position from which the Company faced the outbreak of war.

In March 1939 the Company received another 19 Dennis Lancet IIs, the first five bodied by Park Royal and the remainder by Dennis. The Park Royal design was very distinctive, having a raised roof the full length of the body specifically for the carriage of band instruments. It did not take long before they gained the nickname 'bandwagons'. AJG 44 (without instruments!) is seen postwar on the half-hourly local Canterbury route 29. *W. J. Haynes / Southdown Enthusiasts' Club*

Leyland's answer to the Dennis Ace 20-seater was the Cub, which proved to be its equal, and East Kent ordered six such chassis for delivery in 1939. By this time the Morris Commercials had been withdrawn, but their bodies were found to be still serviceable and in consequence were fitted to the new chassis, Cub AJG 607 seen here receiving the East Kent body from JG 3720. The resultant vehicle looks immaculate, although the small fleetname suggests it was shy to admit that its body was older! It would survive until 1953, by which time the body was 19 years old. *W. J. Haynes / Southdown Enthusiasts' Club*

3. IN THE FRONT LINE
East Kent at war

Anyone who is familiar with the *Dad's Army* feature film will recall the final scene, in which Captain Mainwaring and his men, armed with little more than a fierce determination not to be beaten, stand on the cliffs looking out across the English Channel, with nothing between them and the 'armoured might of the German War Machine'. This was precisely the position in which the East Kent Road Car Company found itself on 3 September 1939.

In actual fact the Company's war work had commenced a couple of days earlier, when some 8,000 schoolchildren, having been evacuated from London by train, were ferried to various locations within its area by East Kent buses. This did not turn out to be a very good idea, however, and by Christmas most had returned home. Indeed, not long afterwards it was the turn of the children of east Kent to be evacuated to safer parts.

The outbreak of World War 2 had profound effects on all bus operators. Places of entertainment were closed, people were advised to stay at home, and the blackout was introduced, bringing its own problems to bus crews. Drivers had to manage with masked headlamps, no street lamps and with familiar landmarks blacked out. Conductors were no better off: interior illumination was by a handful of dim blue bulbs, and conductors, or (more often) 'clippies', would fumble with change and ticket rack whilst holding low-powered torches. Driver-conductors on the one-man-operated 20-seaters probably fared worst of all. Petrol and fuel oil were rationed, supplies being cut by as much as 50%, resulting in severe cuts to services, and East Kent's vehicles had their cream areas repainted grey, to minimise recognition from the air. However, it was soon realised that some of these measures were too severe. Theatres and cinemas reopened to improve public morale, and this brought about an increase in evening traffic. The restrictions on fuel were also relaxed.

Later in the war, as in the previous conflict, some buses were converted to run on producer-gas, in a further effort to save fuel. This time, instead of a balloon on the roof, the gas-producing equipment was mounted on a small trailer which was towed by the vehicle. These conversions, effected not only in east Kent but all over the country, were not really successful. Hill-climbing capabilities in particular were extremely poor, and this precluded the use of such buses in much of the East Kent area.

Almost immediately following the outbreak of war some 30 East Kent coaches, mainly from the 1935 batch of petrol-engined Leyland TS7s, were converted into ambulances and stationed at Ashford, Canterbury and Herne Bay depots. They were manned by East Kent staff for 24 hours a day and retained Company livery. They were intended for civilian use only, and this rule was strictly observed; even during the evacuation of Dunkirk they were not made available for use by the armed forces.

The loss of holiday traffic, cuts in services and the evacuation of civilians meant that the Company was left with a large number of vehicles that were surplus to requirements. Many of these were loaned to other operators throughout the country, wherever they could be gainfully employed. The vehicles concerned were far too numerous and their movements (often from one company to another) too complicated to detail here. However, let us take as an example the AJG-registered batch of 40 Leyland TD5 double-deckers delivered between November 1938 and May 1939. AJG 1 and 2 were sent to East Midland, along with the ex-Thanet Daimlers. AJG 3-10 were loaned to the Lincolnshire Road Car Co, whilst 11-20 went to West Yorkshire. AJG 21-40 were sent along the coast to Southdown, which, in its normal painstaking way, not only painted them in its own livery and numbered them in its own fleet but went as far as fitting them with 'Southdown' radiator badges. AJG 31-5 later moved to Devon General. Other companies to benefit from the hire of East Kent vehicles included Caledonian, Thames Valley, Aldershot & District, City of Oxford and Associated Motorways.

One new vehicle was delivered in 1940, this being BFN 797, a Leyland Tiger TS8 with a Park Royal coach body to a new

enemy air activity to stop them from reaching their destinations. Fifty buses were then despatched to each of the four disembarkation points (the remaining 50 being held in reserve near Canterbury), from where they operated shuttle services to railheads. On at least two occasions, due to a shortage of railway rolling stock, they were required to undertake longer journeys, 40 vehicles being sent to Chatham and 30 to Redhill. Staff worked round the clock, eating at the wheel and sleeping when the opportunity arose. Fortunately, for some unknown reason, the expected air attacks never happened. The exercise ended on 3 June. There are no records of the number of war-weary troops transported during the period, but the numbers were vast. The story of the 'Little Ships' is well documented (and rightly so), but the efforts of the East Kent busmen, equally heroic in their own way, remain unsung.

Following Dunkirk there were several instances of vehicles and drivers being sent to Army units which had no vehicles of their own, usually because they had been abandoned in the retreat from France or Belgium. On these occasions staff slept in their vehicles and ate Army rations, although they continued to be paid by East Kent. Vehicles were also hired by the Ministry of Labour to carry workers to and from the sites where defences against invasion were being built at break-neck speed. Another contract, this time to carry manual workers to and from factories being built in the Midlands, took five open-top double-deckers and 43 Tilling-Stevens single-deckers to a makeshift base near Kidderminster.

Back to the South East. Only a few short weeks after Dunkirk the Luftwaffe began a series of air attacks, firstly on Channel shipping, then on airfields and other strategic sites on the English mainland. Every day one could see British and German aircraft engaged in dogfights over the fields of Kent. On 7 September large formations of German bombers crossed the coast, heading

During World War 2 a number of East Kent vehicles were loaned to other operators to alleviate the vehicle shortages. One such, seen in the wartime livery of Devon General (complete with fleet number DL304), is AJG 34, a 1939 Leyland Titan TD5 with the standard lowbridge Park Royal body of the time. The conductress, the deserted streets and the vehicle's masked lights and white-painted wings complete the picture. *The Omnibus Society*

design owing much to the 1938 body on JG 9944. It featured a curved waistline and a smoother, more curvaceous outline but lacked the glass cant panels and some of the elegance of its 1938 predecessor. It was to have been the prototype for a new generation of luxury coaches but, due to the intervention of the war, remained unique.

Of course, the major event of 1940 was not the delivery of a new coach — even to East Kent — but the evacuation of Dunkirk. On 26 May the War Cabinet, under Winston Churchill, ordered the withdrawal of all British troops from the Continent. Early the following morning the East Kent company was ordered by the Transport Commissioner to provide transport to move the returning troops as quickly as possible from disembarkation points at Dover, Folkestone, Margate and Ramsgate to the nearest railway stations. Some 250 buses were sent to a rendezvous point on the Ashford–Canterbury road, where the drivers were given orders and told to expect heavy

off the radiator. Amazingly, no one else
was injured. In the second incident — also
involving a Daimler — a bomb exploded
close to the rear of the bus as it was leaving
Canterbury, killing the conductress and a
number of passengers. The driver was
injured but managed to help the wounded
from the bus. Although the German aircraft
was still close at hand, another bus was sent
out immediately. It was not compulsory
for crews to work under these conditions
— indeed, the Company even offered to
pay for their evacuation from the Dover
area — but they elected to stay and risk
the constant bombardment and machine-
gunning that faced them daily.

Most of the Company's property suffered
damage of some kind, but Dover, being
so close to the French coast, probably
suffered more than most. One night in
April 1942 a string of bombs was
dropped, one of which landed on an air-raid shelter in which 10
members of staff were taking refuge. Nine were killed. The
garage and office buildings were all destroyed, while the buses
were badly damaged, although these were eventually repaired
and returned to service.

One of the most unusual and most interesting contracts
undertaken during the war was the supply of vehicles to ENSA
(Entertainments National Service Association) for transporting
entertainers around the country to perform for the troops. At the
peak of this contract some 65 coaches were in use.

With the exception of the solitary Leyland TS8 delivered in
1940 no new vehicles had been received since 1939, and,
although service cuts etc had made for a reduced requirement, by
1943 the need for new vehicles was becoming urgent, not least
because of the numbers requisitioned or lost to enemy action.

During the first two years of the war, manufacturers had
continued to build buses, virtually to prewar standards, from
existing stocks of parts; these were known as 'unfrozen', by
virtue of the fact that the stored parts had been 'unfrozen' for
their use. When the parts ran out the Ministry of Supply drew up
specifications for standard single- and double-deck buses that
could be built at minimum cost in terms of both materials and
skilled labour. Aluminium was not to be used in their construction,

for London and bombing the docks on the way. It was the
beginning of daylight bombing raids on London. About a week
later, a huge formation of German bombers with fighter escorts
crossed Kent and bombed London. On their way back towards
the coast they were attacked by the RAF, and the sky was filled
with hundreds of aircraft, some involved in dogfights, while others
fell from the sky in flames. Some 70 German aircraft were shot
down that day. The Battle of Britain had been won.

But it was not only aircraft that presented a threat. Following
the British evacuation from France, the Germans had established
long-range guns on the French coast, clearly visible from Dover,
and cross-Channel shelling became an added hazard, both Dover
and Folkestone being within range. With this form of attack there
could be no warning, unless the day was clear enough to see the
flashes from the guns.

The inability of the bus to hide or retaliate made it fair game
for Luftwaffe pilots, and there were two fatal incidents on the
same day in October 1942. In one a Canterbury-bound Daimler
was attacked near Sturry. The conductress saw sparks coming
from the road and, assuming there was something wrong with
the bus, signalled the driver to stop. However, the bus left the
road and came to rest in a field. A machine-gun bullet had killed
the driver as he sat at the wheel, whilst a cannon shell had blown

leading to considerable increases in weight, and bodies were virtually devoid of such niceties as double-curvature front and rear domes, which required the services of skilled panel-beaters. The resultant vehicles were therefore very angular in appearance. These standard vehicles were to be supplied to all operators, with no individual variations, and specified manufacturers would be appointed to build them.

Guy Motors Ltd, of Wolverhampton, was selected initially as the sole chassis manufacturer. The new chassis was based on Guy's prewar Arab, whose name it perpetuated, and, like its predecessor, it was offered with a 'choice' of either Gardner 5LW or 6LW engine. The word 'choice' is used lightly, for in reality operators had little say in what they received. The Gardner 6LW, being a longer engine, required an extended bonnet, which meant that Mk 1 Arabs so equipped could easily be identified by their protruding radiators. When the Arab II was introduced it was fitted with the longer bonnet, regardless of engine size, so this identifying feature was lost.

Contracts for building the bodywork were awarded to a number of builders, each of which put its own interpretation on the basic design, resulting in some remarkably differing styles. Operators again had no choice in the matter, and, indeed, there seemed little logic in the way the bodies were distributed. Frequently an operator would find itself with a comparatively small batch of vehicles with bodies by several different manufacturers. During the course of the war Southdown received Arabs with bodies by Willowbrook, Strachans, Weymann, Park Royal and Northern Counties, whilst Brighton, Hove & District was allocated just two Arabs, both bodied by Pickering of Scotland. One would have thought that the fuel used in delivery would have been taken into account, if nothing else. East Kent was lucky, for its wartime

In 1943 East Kent took delivery of four Guy Arab IIs with highbridge Park Royal bodywork to utility specification. One of these, BJG 281, is seen on Canterbury city service 27 with a heavy load — one can almost hear the throbbing of the five-cylinder Gardner engine. The full screen display reveals this to be a peacetime scene, completed by the presence of a late-1940s lorry and, in the distance, another Guy Arab. BJG 281 would be withdrawn in 1958 after 15 years' valuable service. *W. J. Haynes / Southdown Enthusiasts' Club*

The war years are almost over in this view of Guy Arab BJG 419 on Folkestone local service 99 to Cheriton, which would serve the army camp at Shorncliffe. By the time this bus was delivered, in January 1945, victory was in sight, which may account for the slight relaxation on the lights, but white paint has nevertheless been applied to the mudguards and skirt to aid visibility. Severe in outline, with angular utility bodywork by Weymann, these buses were a badly needed stopgap, although BJG 419 would not be withdrawn until 1959. Note the sign offering Bed & Breakfast accommodation for 5s! *The Omnibus Society*

Guys were bodied by just two builders. One was Weymann, which (with a few exceptions) built the lowbridge bodies, and the other was East Kent's beloved Park Royal, which concentrated on the highbridge 'deckers.

The first Arabs for East Kent were delivered at the beginning of 1943 in the shape of three Arab Is. Registered BJG 253-5, they had Gardner 5LW engines and highbridge Park Royal bodies with slatted wooden seats, which feature had become standard by that time. They were followed by 11 Arab IIs (BJG 281/2, 301-4/39/53-6) with similar bodywork, delivery of which was spread over a year from June 1943. In November 1944 delivery commenced of no fewer than 45 Arab IIs (BJG 400-44), this time with 55-seat lowbridge bodies by Weymann, which showed a return to upholstered seats. The final utility Guys, delivered later in 1945, consisted of BJG 461/2, with highbridge Park Royal bodies, BJG 472/5, the only ones to receive highbridge bodies by Weymann, and BJG 473/4, also bodied by Weymann but to lowbridge configuration. The majority of the wartime Guys were fitted with the Gardner 5LW engine, but 15 had the larger, six-cylinder version.

A small number of chassis were rebodied with single-deck bodies to utility specification, all of which were built by H. V. Burlingham of Blackpool. Three of these bodies were fitted to the original open-top TS1s already mentioned, the others being replacements for war-damaged single-deck bodies.

Late in 1944 the capture of the German gun sites brought an end to the shelling of the Kent coast, but a new threat took its place in the shape of the V2 rocket. However, peace eventually came in May 1945, and the Company was able to set about the task of restoring things to normal.

4. RENEWAL, REPAIR, RECONSTRUCTION
A story of recovery

The end of the war found the East Kent fleet sadly depleted due to requisitioning and war losses. Of those buses that remained many were overdue for withdrawal and all were suffering from a lack of proper maintenance. Replacement of worn-out and bomb-damaged vehicles was a priority. However, operators all over the country were in the same position. Materials were still in short supply and established manufacturers were unable to meet the demand. As a result countless small concerns which had been engaged in building lorry bodies, high-class cars or even aircraft production saw a lucrative opening and began to build bus and coach bodies. Names such as Portsmouth Aviation, Gurney Nutting, Windover and Mann Egerton started to appear on coachbuilders' plates.

Many companies turned wherever they could to obtain new vehicles. To use Southdown as an example once more, its first postwar coaches were bodied by Duple, Windover, Park Royal and Eastern Coach Works as well as its usual choice of Harrington and Beadle. East Kent, however, rather shot itself in the foot by remaining steadfastly faithful to Park Royal, at least for its coaches. In September 1945 some 50 Leyland Tiger coaches and 60 Dennis Lancet single-deck buses were ordered, all with Park Royal bodies, of which just four coaches were received in 1946, the rest being delivered through 1947 and 1948. The first of the Dennis Lancets did not arrive until 1947, the last of the order arriving in 1949, some four years after the end of the war.

The Dennis Lancets, although classified as Lancet IIIs, were little different from their prewar counterparts. They were registered CFN 110-69, although 111-21 were actually the last to be delivered, arriving in mid-1949. CFN 110 was fitted with the 1934 Park Royal body from Tilling-Stevens FN 9007, and it was originally intended that CFN 111-21 would also be given bodies of 1933/4 vintage from Tilling-Stevens B10s. Following the experiment with CFN 110, however, the plan was abandoned, and the 1933/4 bodies went instead onto 1936 Dennis Lancets in the JG 68xx series.

During the war Leyland had been engaged in building military vehicles, particularly tanks, for which it had developed a new engine, designated E181. With the war over it was the E181 engine that Leyland decided to fit into its postwar bus and coach range. The double-decker was classified PD1 (Passenger Double-deck 1), the single-deck chassis, not surprisingly, becoming the PS1. The six-cylinder engine was of only 7.4 litres' capacity — only slightly larger than the Gardner 5LW — and anyone who has ridden on a PD1 or PS1 will recall the painfully slow juddering tickover, which gave the impression that it was about to stall at every turn. Nevertheless, large numbers of both types were built and sold by Leyland, and, although never renowned for their sprightliness, they fulfilled a need at a time when buses were difficult to obtain, and most enjoyed a decent lifespan.

The PS1 was the chassis chosen by East Kent for its postwar coach fleet — not really surprising, as this was the natural

In the years 1947-9 East Kent took delivery of 60 Park Royal-bodied Dennis Lancet IIIs which closely resembled their prewar cousins. Dating from 1949, 35-seat CFN 113 is seen in Ashford, where Maidstone & District's garage appears to have had a 'once over' — possibly a case of 'If East Kent can do it, so can we!'.
Glyn Kraemer-Johnson collection

Representing the 1948 deliveries is CFN 169, a Dennis Lancet III with rear-entrance Park Royal body. This front nearside view somehow emphasises the vehicle's aged appearance, but the type was certainly not short of admirers. *Eric Surfleet / D. Clark collection, courtesy Southdown Enthusiasts' Club*

The combination of Leyland Tiger PS1 chassis and Park Royal bodywork, exemplified here by CFN 76, produced a true classic coach, an already pleasing effect being enhanced by the rich red and cream of East Kent. Delivered in 1947, these vehicles were used on express work as well as excursions as here. One could join an excursion to Canterbury for 5s (25p) or to Herne Bay for 6s (30p). *W. J. Haynes / Southdown Enthusiasts' Club*

A scene recorded on 5 June 1952, when the photographer was aiming to capture the dying hours of London's trams without sparing a thought for East Kent's Leyland Tiger PS1 coaches, although these too are now but a memory. Followed by another from the same batch, CFN 106 heels to the offside as it speeds through Lee Green and on towards Victoria Coach Station. *R. W. A. Jones / Online Transport Archive / Photobus*

successor to the prewar TS8. The 32-seat rear-entrance Park Royal bodywork was basically similar to the prewar version, with straight waistrail and few of the graceful curves that had distinguished BFN 797. These vehicles retained the prewar livery of two-tone red and cream and were registered CFN 60-109. Express services having been reinstated in 1946, and with holidaymakers and day-trippers returning to the seaside resorts, coaches were much in demand, and it was a pity that the Company had to wait so long for delivery to be completed.

With double-deckers East Kent was a little more fortunate. Fifty Leyland Titan PDs were ordered in September 1946, and (the Company's beloved Park Royal for once being forsaken) Leyland's own 53-seat lowbridge bodywork was specified. Delivered in 1947/8, 49 of these buses (CJG 938-86) were PD1As, differing from the standard PD1 only in having Metalastik rubber bushes in the suspension, but CJG 987, delivered in 1948, was of type PD2/1. Successor to the PD1, this had Leyland's new O.600 engine of 9.8 litres; far more powerful than the PD2, the PD2 was to become one of the all-time classic British bus chassis. The management at East Kent was apparently unimpressed, however, for the bus remained unique in the fleet.

To extend the life of the existing double-deck fleet, the Company had a number of TD4s and TD5s rebodied in 1948/9. Twenty-four received 55-seat lowbridge bodies by Eastern Coach Works to that coachbuilder's standard design, then being delivered in large numbers (mainly on Bristol chassis) to Tilling Group operators throughout the country. Of totally standard appearance, they were fitted with the standard ECW

With a typical Kent advertisement — for Whitbread's Ale & Stout — Guy Arab II BJG 356 heads through Canterbury on service 23A, followed by Park Royal-bodied Leyland Tiger PS1 CFN 71. Delivered with a Gardner 5LW five-cylinder engine, the Arab would never be fitted with a 6LW, confining it to city routes in Canterbury, these being comparatively flat. After withdrawal in 1958 it would pass to the Llandudno & Colwyn Bay Electric Railway, joining similar Southdown vehicles in replacing the last of the trams. *W. J. Haynes / Southdown Enthusiasts' Club*

In 1947/8 Leyland supplied 50 lowbridge Titans, these comprising 49 PD1s and a lone PD2. To the casual observer they were very similar vehicles, even to painted radiators and continuous number sequence, but the offside wing protruding from the front panel on the PD2 gave the game away. Here PD1 CJG 986 looks the part outside the Rose & Crown, Elham, in company with a prewar classic car. The advertisement (on the board of the public house) offering hunting accommodation would provoke controversy today. *The Omnibus Society*

A question frequently asked of bus photographers is: 'Why do you take pictures of modern buses?' The answer is they are only new once, as was the case in 1948 with CJG 987.
The only Leyland PD2/1 in the fleet, this had lowbridge Leyland bodywork.
The presence of the Nuffield emblem reminds us that this view pre-dates Morris's merger with Austin; given East Kent's experience prewar with Morris products it is perhaps surprising that it should accept such advertisements! Note the Leyland Cub in the background. *The Omnibus Society*

By the end of World War 2 the bodywork on the Leyland TD4s was time-expired but the chassis themselves were still capable of giving good service, so these were overhauled and rebodied. The first of the 1936 batch, JG 8201, received a new lowbridge body by Eastern Coach Works in 1948, being seen here *c*1960 pulling out from the kerb past a very 1950s Bedford Dormobile and being pursued by a new Jaguar Mk II motor car while on Canterbury city service 24. *Photobus*

sliding vents instead of the usual half-drop windows favoured by East Kent. The ECW body sat comfortably on the TD chassis and looked well in East Kent's attractive livery.

In 1949 a further 35 TD4s and TD5s were rebodied, this time by . . . you've guessed it — Park Royal! These too were of lowbridge layout but seated the more usual 53. The bodies provided were rather strange; although by this time Park Royal had reverted to a more curvaceous design (influenced more than a little by the London RT, of which it was building hundreds), these were to an almost semi-utility design, angular in appearance and with deep metal louvres over the side windows. This impression was heightened by the fitting of opening vents to the front windows of the type used on the utility Guys. However, the provision of these bodies gave the buses greatly extended lives, the last not being withdrawn until as late as 1963, by which time some of the chassis were 27 years old.

A further exercise in modernisation commenced in 1950 and amounted to an early example of recycling. To help ease the vehicle shortage Beadle had come up with an idea whereby the engine and running units from a time-expired prewar vehicle was incorporated into a new integral (or 'chassisless') body structure. The 'Beadle Rebuild', as it became known, proved

popular with a number of BET operators, especially in the South East. To evaluate the idea East Kent sent the chassis of three Leyland TD5s, AJG 1-3, to Dartford; these returned in 1951 as 35-seat coaches FFN 445-7, following which a further 25 chassis from the same batch of TD5s were despatched to be similarly treated, materialising in 1952 as GFN 256-80.

The rebuilt vehicles had full fronts but with a bulkhead behind the driver and a forward entrance behind the front wheel. Whilst the general body style was quite pleasant, with more than a hint of what was to follow on underfloor-engined chassis, the frontal treatment was not overly attractive. However, to the general public a full front meant a modern vehicle, and that was what it was all about. These useful little vehicles were quite long-lived, many lasting until the mid-'Sixties.

The final group of vehicles to be replaced in the late 'Forties comprised the 20-seat Dennis Aces bought for use on routes in more sparsely populated areas. Dating from 1934/5, these were now well past their prime, and to replace them the Company purchased 15 Dennis Falcons. Powered by the Gardner 4LK diesel engine, these again were of normal-control (bonneted) layout, but their 20-seat Dennis bodies were of more stylish (if still rather dated) appearance. They were also larger and would eventually be upseated to 29. Equipped for one-person operation, they were registered EFN 556-70.

In the spring of 1950 were delivered what would be the last half-cab coaches bought new by the Company, in the shape of 25 Dennis Lancet IIIs with 32-seat Park Royal coach bodywork. Like the Beadle rebuilds these featured a forward-entrance layout. They also introduced a new coach livery, with greater areas of cream, together with a new fleetname in script, but both were short-lived. The bodywork differed quite markedly from what had gone before: the rear end tapered inwards, and they had three large side windows, each divided by a slim silver pillar; the most obvious difference was at the front, however, for they had only a very short canopy over the bonnet — just enough to house a destination screen — instead of the usual full canopy. Registration numbers followed on from the Falcons, being EFN 571-95. Sadly they were obsolete almost as soon as they were delivered, for the underfloor-engined chassis was on the horizon, and many were later downgraded to bus duties.

By the beginning of the new decade the ravages of war had been virtually overcome, and the fleet was once more up to strength and ready to cope with the ever-increasing holiday traffic, which was shortly to reach its peak.

For its rural routes East Kent needed smaller vehicles and must have had visions of the prewar Dennis Aces by placing into service 15 Dennis Falcons, with 20-seat Dennis bodywork, in 1949/50. Later upseated to accommodate 29, they were to last 17 years before withdrawal, in 1967; here EFN 564 on the 31 Faversham–Chilham route meets a 1966 AEC Regent V on route 1 at Chilham. Fortunately EFN 568 would pass into preservation and can nowadays be seen regularly on the rally circuit, reliving the glory days. *The M&D and East Kent Bus Club*

To help fulfil their postwar coaching needs three BET operators in the South East — Southdown, Maidstone & District and East Kent — turned to Beadle of Dartford, which was producing quite presentable semi-chassisless vehicles based on reusable prewar running units. East Kent's examples used parts from its AJG-registered Leyland Titan TD5s. Seen at Hastings, GFN 278 was delivered in 1952 and, in common with the rest of its batch, would last until the mid-1960s. *Eric Surfleet / D. Clark collection, courtesy Southdown Enthusiasts' Club*

East Kent coaches everywhere, but taking pride of place is EFN 579, a Dennis Lancet III with 32-seat Park Royal coachwork. The large radiator dates the coach but nevertheless imbues it with so much character. With the advent of sleeker, underfloor-engined coaches these vehicles would soon be outdated but nevertheless gave sterling service, the last not being withdrawn until 1967. *Glyn Kraemer-Johnson collection*

29

5. ALL CHANGE!

Changes of allegiance — and engine position

Given East Kent's satisfaction prewar with the Leyland Titan TD4 and TD5 and its purchase postwar of further Leyland products, it might have been expected that future deliveries would be Leylands. However, in 1950 the Company pressed ahead with an order for 80 Guy Arab IIIs, albeit still with the tried and tested Park Royal bodywork. The first 40, with lowbridge bodywork to 7ft 6in width, are represented here by EFN 188, seen in Canterbury bus station in 1951. *Geoff Rixon*

The PD1s (and solitary PD2) were the last Leyland double-deckers purchased by East Kent, at least during the period covered by this book. Those who mattered, just like those who mattered in a number of other companies, had been very impressed with the rugged reliability of the Guy Arab that had been thrust upon them during the war years — so much so that an order was placed for no fewer than 80 Arab IIIs with Gardner 6LW engines and Park Royal 53-seat lowbridge bodies. The first 40 of these, EFN 170-209, were delivered in the first part of 1950 and carried the same style of 'semi-utility' bodywork as the rebodied TD4s and TD5s. They nevertheless proved themselves capable workhorses and operated throughout the East Kent area.

As it happened the 1950 Arabs proved to be East Kent's last lowbridge double-deckers, the Company taking advantage of a delay in the delivery of the remaining 40 vehicles by changing the bodywork order to one for highbridge 56-seaters. These materialised in 1951 as FFN 360-99 and were totally different from the previous year's deliveries. The design was based very much on the London RT, with curved frontal profile, four-bay construction and winding half-drop windows with radiused corners. The low radiator and bonnet line of the Guy suited the design well, although for some strange reason the front bulkhead window was much higher than was necessary, unlike that on the RT. Push-out vents replaced the wartime type on the front windows, and the whole resulted in some very attractive vehicles. They were also East Kent's first 8ft-wide double-deckers.

A follow-up order called for a further 30 Guys, this time of the updated Arab IV model. The body on the first of the batch (GFN 908) was actually built by Guy on Park Royal frames (although, apart from a straight lower edge to the windscreen and not having platform doors, it was barely distinguishable from the rest). This came about because the body had been built in 1950 on an Arab III chassis for Newport Corporation and had been exhibited at the 1950 Commercial Motor Show; Newport subsequently cancelled its order, so the body was transferred to the first of the East Kent order, in which form it was exhibited at the 1952 Show!

EAST KENT

RELIEF 3

NSTON, ACOL
MINSTER
CANTERBURY 59

JG 7028

EFN 198

EAST KENT

FFN 374

The rest of the batch (GFN 909-37) was delivered in 1953 with the anticipated highbridge Park Royal bodywork. This was virtually identical to that on the FFN-registered batch but with the addition of platform doors, the main difference being that the chassis were fitted with the newly introduced New Look front or 'tin front', as it was irreverently known. On most chassis types the introduction of the concealed radiator was generally agreed to be a retrograde step, at least as far as appearance was concerned. However, the version fitted to the Guy (and the Daimler, for they were virtually identical) was a neat and not too ungainly unit which, in this writer's opinion at least, was as pleasing to the eye as was the exposed radiator. The GFNs were mainly associated with the Thanet services until replaced by AEC Regents in 1959.

With its graceful, no-nonsense lines, Park Royal bodywork was very much the standard choice for East Kent. By the time this photograph was taken in the early 1950s the new bus station had opened in Canterbury, providing a marvellous opportunity to compare similar bodywork on different types of chassis. On the left is JG 7028, a rebodied Leyland Titan TD4, while on the right and still quite new is Guy Arab III EFN 198, the differing treatment of cab and wings radically altering the appearance. *Simon Butler*

In 1951 East Kent received the balance of its order for 80 Guy Arab IIIs, these having fundamental differences which made them quite distinct from the previous batch — principally that they were built to highbridge layout and 8ft width. There was more than a hint of London Transport RTW, with four-bay window layout on the lower deck, raked front and upright rear, while the eventual fitment of a Gardner 6LW engine made for a very dependable machine. Seen on the main Isle of Thanet route linking Ramsgate with Margate is FFN 374. *Alan Cross*

31

The need for further new buses to replace ageing prewar vehicles led to the delivery in 1953 of 30 more Guy Arabs, this time of the new Mk IV version, with highbridge Park Royal bodywork. The most noticeable difference concerns the restyled front, minus the distinctive Guy radiator, although Guy's 'Indian Chief' was incorporated into the design. With a Maidstone & District Beadle Rebuild in the background, GFN 936 is seen in Maidstone on the lengthy route 67 to Canterbury, operated jointly with Maidstone & District.
Eric Surfleet / D. Clark collection, courtesy Southdown Enthusiasts' Club

Highbridge Guy Arab IV/Park Royal MFN 886 looks every inch of its 8ft width when compared with lowbridge Arab III EFN 178 alongside, at Canterbury in the early 1960s. By this time the AEC Regent V was starting to make its presence felt, but for now it was still possible to savour the sound of Gardner engines!
John Bishop

The march of modern architecture in bomb-damaged Canterbury and the appearance of nationally known High Street names were well underway when this view was recorded of nearly new Guy Arab IV MFN 897 with highbridge Park Royal bodywork. Delivered in 1956/7, these supremely well-proportioned buses represented the apogee of East Kent double-deck design.
Omnibus Society

Three years would elapse before any further double-deckers were received, but in 1956 came the first of 20 Guy Arab IVs with 61-seat Park Royal bodies, again equipped with platform doors. By this time the Park Royal body had evolved, and, although its RT ancestry was still evident, the Park Royal designers had, if anything, improved on that classic design. MFN 883-907 perpetuated the New Look front and were fitted with sliding ventilators on all main windows, which gave them an even sleeker appearance; as suggested in the Introduction, in the authors' opinions these were just about the most handsome buses ever built. They were generally associated with Dover depot. They say you should quit while

you're on top, and that's just what East Kent did, for these were the last Guys to join the fleet.

Meanwhile the underfloor-engined coach had made its appearance. All the major manufacturers of 'heavyweight' chassis had introduced underfloor-engined models for single-deck and coach bodywork, and the design had been accepted almost universally. With the engine placed amidships under the floor the whole of the vehicle's length was available for seating. This generally meant an increase of between eight and 10 seats, which meant an increase of 8-10 fare-paying passengers. It also meant that the door could be positioned at the front, ahead of the front wheels, so that the driver could collect fares, but initially most had centre or rear entrances. In 1951 the conductor's job still seemed secure.

East Kent's first venture into underfloor-engined chassis was a cautious one, being limited to six Leyland Royal Tigers with centre-entrance coach bodywork by Park Royal. The first three (FFN 448-50), for touring work, seated 30, the remaining trio (FFN 451-3) 37. Most coachbuilders seemed to have similar ideas for their first coach bodies on underfloor-engined chassis — straight roof and waistline, centre entrance and lots of decorative brightwork that tended to give a slightly transatlantic

In 1953 East Kent took delivery of two 'flagship' vehicles in the form of two more Leyland Royal Tigers, this time with Duple Ambassador coachwork. Here HFN 2 displays the modernised 'East Kent' fleetname slanting towards the rear. With seating for just 32 passengers, the pair were used almost exclusively on touring work for 10 years. Both would be withdrawn in 1967. *The Omnibus Society*

In 1954, following the move to underfloor engines, East Kent returned to Dennis Bros for its coaching requirements, taking no fewer than 30 Lancet UF models with attractive Duple Ambassador IV bodywork. Seen in Folkestone bus station is HJG 15. The highbridge Guy Arab IV in the background, MFN 888, is now fully preserved and a welcome sight at rallies. *The Omnibus Society*

look. Park Royal was no exception, although the curved mouldings around the wheel-arches seemed to be a throwback to the half-cab. Nevertheless, in their smart livery of two-tone red and cream they were impressive-looking coaches. Almost unbelievably, they were also the first vehicles in the East Kent fleet to boast saloon heaters!

The Beadle rebuilds had boosted the coach fleet to an acceptable level, so there was no need to rush headlong into placing orders for underfloor-engined chassis, and just two more Leyland Royal Tigers were ordered. However, the estimated delivery time was so long that the Company took the rather surprising step of purchasing two petrol-engined Bedford SBs for touring work. They were delivered with Duple Vega bodies only partially completed and were finished as 28-seaters by East Kent itself, hence there were differences from the standard Duple body. The Bedford was a front-engined chassis, but to compete with the new underfloor-engined heavyweights a full-front body was fitted as standard. Duple's offering was a rather bulbous affair, again with a hint of contemporary American car design about it. GFN 600/1 served as touring coaches until the end of 1955, when they were demoted to excursion work, having their seating capacity increased to 35. They were withdrawn in 1963, and GFN 600 initially survived in preservation.

The two delayed Royal Tigers arrived in May 1953 and had the privilege of being registered HFN 1 and 2, these being the days before cherished numberplates. These too had Duple bodywork, but this was far superior to that on the Bedfords. Known as the 'Coronation Ambassador', the design was basically Duple's 'Ambassador' given a lot more chrome embellishment and renamed for Coronation year. Seating 32, they had centre entrances. The centre entrance on underfloor-engined chassis was a popular feature with both coach and bus passengers, for it allowed two lucky individuals to sit 'up front' beside the driver . . . and, if you were a spotty-faced bus enthusiast in short trousers, you might even get to speak to him — an honour indeed! The delay in the delivery of these coaches probably did Leyland Motors little good, for these would be the last new Leylands to be bought by East Kent until the advent of the National Bus Company.

Thirty more Duple Ambassador bodies were ordered for delivery in 1954, but these were mounted on Dennis

Lancet UF underfloor-engined chassis. The Lancet UF was not a marked success; in fact the East Kent coaches formed the largest single order for the type. In a rare instance of two batches of vehicle being registered in a continuous sequence they materialised as HJG 3-32, the first six being 32-seat tourers, the remainder seating 41. All had centre entrances.

Meanwhile, in 1953, two small independents had been acquired. One was 'Enterprise' (Saxby & Sons) of Margate, the second Sarjeant Bros of Cheriton. With these came four Bedford/Duple OBs and, from Enterprise, OKE 470, a Bedford SB with 32-seat Plaxton body but basically similar to GFN 600/1. The Bedford OB, usually with Duple Vista coach body, was a normal-control petrol-engined 29-seater synonymous with the independent coach operator during the 'Forties and 'Fifties — everyone had at least one! Surprisingly, given that they were non-standard, East Kent kept all four. They were usually to be found on excursion work, but on summer Saturdays they would frequently be pressed into service on London express work. The OBs all survived until 1957, the SB until 1963.

Possibly the most popular coach of the immediate postwar period was the Duple-bodied Bedford OB, used by many a private and public company alike. East Kent had four, all acquired from smaller operators, including MKK 40, which came from A. Saxby & Sons Ltd (trading as 'Enterprise'), Margate, in 1953. The line-up behind it in this view includes a Beadle Rebuild, an Eastern Coach Works-bodied Leyland Titan and, on the far right, a Leyland Tiger PS1 (CFN 88). *J. T. Wilson / Southdown Enthusiasts' Club*

The year 1955 saw further changes in manufacturer, one of which was to prove something of a milestone.

Following the success of its chassisless coaches using prewar running units, Beadle of Dartford had joined forces with fellow Rootes Group company Commer Cars of Luton to build modern integral buses and coaches. These innovative vehicles used the Commer TS3 engine, which in itself was unusual, being a horizontal three-cylinder two-stroke (as indicated by its designation, although there were those who claimed that the 'TS' stood for 'Tilling-Stevens', in whose old Maidstone factory the engines were built). The Beadle-Commer integral was bought in reasonable numbers by various BET companies, Southdown taking three batches totalling 25 vehicles that were the mainstay of its London express services for several years. East Kent purchased just three: KFN 250-2 were front-entrance 41-seaters and were classified as dual-purpose vehicles, although they were rarely used on stage-carriage work. To the best of the writer's knowledge the only time this happened was during the Suez Crisis of 1956, when fuel was in short supply and the Beadle-Commers were put onto bus work because of their remarkably low fuel consumption. The Commer TS3 would

In 1952 East Kent took into stock two Bedford SB Duple Vega-bodied coaches for touring work. The following year it acquired another Bedford SB, this time with Plaxton Venturer coachwork, from the business of A. Saxby & Sons Ltd. OKE 470, pictured *en route* to London with a good load, would see 10 years' service with East Kent, surviving until 1963. *Roy Marshall collection / East Pennine Transport Group*

frequently return 20mpg — virtually double that of most comparable diesel engines. On the downside, the Beadle-Commer was hardly the quietest of vehicles, and its sound was unmistakable. It had a throaty roar accompanied by a rasping exhaust, which together sounded rather like a bucketful of wasps — and it was lovely! The bodywork on these coaches was to a simple and attractive design and was to become a familiar sight throughout east Kent, despite the fact that KFN 250-2 were to remain unique.

The other new arrivals in 1955 were also dual-purpose vehicles — 40 AEC Reliances with 41-seat front-entrance bodywork by Weymann (KFN 210-49). The first 20 were fitted with the 7.7-litre AEC AV470 engine, the remainder having the AV410, of only 6.75 litres (although these latter would have this replaced by the larger unit later in life). From the start KFN 240-9 were fitted-out for one-man operation (as it was then called), and the rest were similarly equipped during 1957/8. A further 20 similar vehicles (LJG 305-26), all with the AV470 engine, were delivered in 1956. Initially used as coaches, they too were converted for OMO in 1957/8.

The Weymann-bodied Reliances were long-lived, some lasting for 20 years. For a long time they were the mainstay of the South Coast Express service, but they were just as happy tootling around country lanes on rural bus routes. However, perhaps their greatest significance was that with the delivery of these vehicles AEC became the major supplier of chassis for coaches and single-deck buses — a situation that, not long afterwards, would apply to double-deckers as well.

In your authors' opinions 1957 witnessed the zenith of British bus design, with some of the all-time classic buses and coaches entering service. Mention has already been made of the MFN-registered Guy Arabs, so, before the drooling starts all over again, let us move on to the touring coaches delivered that year — and the drooling can start all over again!

Beadle had updated the design of its integral, naming it the 'Rochester'. This featured a distinctive curve to the front side windows and the rear of the driver's cab window and had more decorative mouldings. It was this design that formed the basis for MJG 41-52, 32-seat AEC Reliance 470s, but these also had glass quarterlights in the roof and a blue-tinted sun visor, which gave them a distinctly continental appearance. By this time most operators were standardising on the front entrance, even for coaches, so the centre door on these was quite unusual. Finished in East Kent's superb cherry red with a broad cream waistband, they were exceptionally handsome vehicles. Unfortunately they were later subjected to various livery changes, including red and grey, and when some received NBC dual-purpose livery of poppy red and white . . . well, the less said the better.

At the same time as the touring coaches came 16 dual-purpose vehicles, and these were followed later in the year by a further 23. These too were Beadle-bodied AEC Reliances, MJG 285-300 being 37-seaters, NFN 327-49 seating 41. The front-entrance bodywork was virtually identical to that on the Beadle-Commers KFN 250-2, without the embellishments of the touring coaches. MJG 285/6, 300 were delivered in pale blue Europabus livery receiving fleet livery in 1961. All were used initially as coaches, but in the mid-'Sixties they were equipped for OMO and downgraded to bus status.

The AEC era had begun.

The large batch of Weymann-bodied AEC Reliances delivered in 1955 seemed almost indestructible, some seeing 20 years' service. Pictured in the 1960s on the seafront at Hastings, East Sussex, KFN 216 is working a local service to Pett and would have been based at East Kent's small Hastings garage. The trolleybuses have already gone but the cliff railway to Hastings Castle in the background survives to this day. *The M&D and East Kent Bus Club*

Clearly satisfied with the dual-purpose Weymann-bodied AEC Reliances delivered in 1955/6, East Kent was prompted to order another 12 Reliances, this time with Beadle coach bodywork. Delivered in 1957, MJG 47 is seen when new on a tour to the Lake District and Royal Deeside. With seating for 32 passengers these vehicles must have been the last word in comfort, which fact, coupled with their immaculate paintwork, made them truly fine vehicles and a credit to East Kent. *Roy Marshall / Bristol Vintage Bus Group*

6. THE AEC YEARS
The Three 'Rs' — Regents, Reliances and . . . er, Bridgemasters!

The Weymann- and Beadle-bodied Reliances had established the AEC as the new standard chassis for single-deck buses and coaches, and in 1959 the set was completed with the arrival of 40 72-seat Park Royal-bodied AEC Regent Vs, fitted with the AEC AV590 9.6-litre engine. Since the increase in the maximum permitted length of double-deckers to 30ft it had become quite normal for operators to specify forward entrances, which enabled the driver to supervise loading and unloading, leaving the conductor free to concentrate on collecting fares, and this was the layout chosen by East Kent for its Regents. They had sliding (rather than the more usual jack-knife) doors, and the bodywork was full-fronted with full-width cabs, a style then popular in some quarters, notably fellow BET operators Ribble and Southdown. The Park Royal body was still attractive, especially when compared with some of the rear-engined 'deckers then entering service elsewhere, or even nearby Southdown's 'Queen Mary' PD3s. The gracefully curving front of Park Royal's earlier designs may have been forsaken for a more upright profile, but somehow the inclusion of the standard Regent V radiator grille and a gently curving lower edge to the windscreen created an appearance less aggressive than that of Southdown's Leylands. They were registered PFN 843-82, from which they quickly gained the nickname of 'Puffins'. PFN 843 appeared at the 1958 Commercial Motor Show, and the writer's enduring memory from that occasion is of an uncomfortably narrow staircase. However, this was rectified, and the rest of the batch were given wider staircases. All 40 'Puffins' were allocated initially to Thanet. In due course the entrance position would make these buses suitable candidates to be adapted for what was then known universally as one-man operation (OMO), half a dozen being so modified in 1971.

The dual-purpose vehicle was now, quite logically, the standard single-decker, and two batches totalling 60 vehicles were delivered in 1960/1. Registered TFN 400-39, VJG 500 and WFN

501-18, they had 41-seat bodywork, this time by Park Royal. This was of a new design featuring twin flat glass windscreens, an ornamental grille that varied in shape between the batches and a side moulding that curved gently down towards the rear. It also introduced a new type of ventilator in place of the usual sliders; known as the Auster Duovent, this consisted of two angled glasses that formed a triangle, the lower one opening inwards to provide what was claimed to be draught-free ventilation.

As a result of experiments carried out on three of the NFN-registered Beadle Reliances, the TFNs carried a new livery style. This was basically all-over cream with red dash and lower side panels within the mouldings. The scheme was not found acceptable, however, and was modified to include a red waistband and boot doors, in which form it became standard.

The surprise delivery of 1960 was TJG 440. The only coach delivered that year, this was a Ford Thames Trader 570E with 41-seat Harrington Crusader coachwork. It could hardly have been less standard, but it would nevertheless remain in the fleet until 1972.

The AEC Regent V had now become the standard double-decker, a further 16 arriving in 1961. These marked a return to half-cab layout, with the usual AEC bonnet and grille, and again carried 72-seat forward-entrance bodywork by Park Royal, this time with folding jack-knife doors. However, apart from the seating capacity and entrance position, they had little in common with the PFNs, being based on the ugly slab-sided, square-box design used on rear-engined chassis. The upper- and lower-deck windows were of unequal depth, and the body had frameless single-skin domes. Even the superb East Kent livery seemed to do little to improve their

Even from the offside there was no disguising that Park Royal-bodied AEC Regent V PFN 882 was a forward-entrance vehicle, the staircase panel behind the driver's cab giving the game away. Numerically the last of its batch, it is seen at the entrance to Canterbury bus station in the 1960s. Withdrawn in 1976, it would remain in stock until 1977, when it moved to Eastbourne to launch a local bus company, Cavendish Coaches, based near the then home of one of the authors. *Eric Surfleet / D. Clark collection, courtesy Southdown Enthusiasts' Club*

East Kent vehicle policy continued to favour AEC in 1960, when 40 dual-purpose Park Royal-bodied Reliances were purchased. With a cream roof and stylised moulding, these would represent East Kent not only throughout the 1960s but into the '70s as well. Numerically the last of the batch, newly delivered TFN 439 is seen on the L5 Herne Bay–London service. *Eric Surfleet / D. Clark collection, courtesy Southdown Enthusiasts' Club*

AEC Regent V/Park Royal WFN 831 stands proudly under the clock at Canterbury bus station when almost new. Delivered in 1961, this was one of a batch of 16 — all fitted with illuminated offside advertisement panels — which differed in body style from the initial batch of 1958/9 and set the pattern for future deliveries of the type. *Eric Surfleet / D. Clark collection, courtesy Southdown Enthusiasts' Club*

This view of 6799 FN, one of the fourth batch of AEC Regent Vs with Park Royal bodywork, seems to accentuate the type's very upright appearance, but it is heartening to note the full blind display, given the limited information by now being supplied by many other operators. The bus is seen on Thanet route 49 in the early 1970s; note the traditional East Kent bus stop still in use at this time. One wonders if the pedestrians have visited the Brown Jug public house on the left! *The M&D and East Kent Bus Club*

appearance (although when they later appeared in NBC poppy red it became apparent just how much the cherry red and ivory had helped!). Could these buses really have come from the same stable as the MFN Guy Arabs?

Love them or loathe them, more half-cab Regents were on the way, and by 1968 there were 121 in the fleet, differing only in minor detail. For instance the first two (1961 and 1962) batches (WFN 827-42 and YJG 810-26) were fitted with illuminated offside advert panels, another 'fad' of the time that never really took off and abandoned on the 1963 deliveries (6783-6805 FN). AFN 763-82B of 1964 and all subsequent Regents (including GJG 733-62D of 1966) boasted fluorescent lighting, whilst the final batch (MFN 938-52F) were 8ft 2½in wide and had the AV690 engine of 11.3 litres.

Although the EFN-registered Guys had been the last lowbridge 'deckers to be bought, there remained one service for which they were still needed. This was the 129, a Dover local route, which passed under a low bridge in Coombe Valley Road and required the use of double-deckers. The problem was solved in 1962 by the purchase of three AEC Bridgemasters (YJG 807-9). AEC's answer to the Bristol Lodekka (introduced in 1954 as the first low-height double-decker with a central gangway on both decks but available only to nationalised companies), the Bridgemaster was an integral AEC/Park Royal product, the bodywork being not dissimilar to that on the half-cab Regent Vs, though the low overall height meant that the windows on the lower deck were the same depth as those upstairs, which helped the overall appearance a little.

The year 1962 also saw the arrival of the first 36ft

coaches, in the shape of 20 AEC Reliances with Park Royal 46-seat bodywork. Registered 519-38 FN, they were fitted with the more powerful 9.6-litre AV590 engine. Twelve of these coaches were delivered in the pale blue Europabus livery. The bodywork, whilst not unattractive, was basically to the standard BET bus style with a revised front end and additional mouldings (which might account for the fact that the entire batch would receive new Plaxton Panorama Elite 49-seat coach bodies in 1972/3). Another 10 similar coaches were delivered the following year, but with 49-seat bodies; they were registered 6539-48 FN — another rare example of registration numbers following on from a previous batch (and these too would all be rebodied by Plaxton, in 1974). Between 1964 and 1966 the Company took delivery of a further three batches of similar coaches, totalling 48 vehicles (AFN 596-605B, DJG 606-31C, GJG 632-43D). These differed from the earlier coaches in having larger windows (four per side) with fixed glass and forced ventilation. They also had power-operated doors, which made them more suitable for use on bus work when the time came.

Twelve new touring coaches purchased in 1964 brought a new type of body into the fleet. This was the Duple Commander, a body being supplied to a number of BET fleets at the time, including Maidstone & District and Southdown. East Kent's had 34 seats and were on AEC Reliance chassis with the AH470 7.7-litre engine. Registrations were AFN 488-99B.

Since the introduction of the underfloor engine all single-deckers supplied to East Kent had been to dual-purpose specification (*i.e.* a bus body with coach seats), but a batch of four Reliances

East Kent turned to Duple's Commander for the bodywork of 12 AEC Reliance touring coaches delivered in 1964. Seen in the early 1970s, awaiting passengers for another tour at Canterbury bus station, AFN 497B still looks the part; note that even after 10 years the bumper still sparkles, while the brightwork has avoided the attentions of over-zealous painters. *John Bishop*

In 1965 East Kent took delivery of four AEC Reliances with Marshall bus bodywork, although the chassis had been completed to full coach specification. One of the quartet, DJG 357C, is seen still at Deal on 25 January 1975, its traditional livery comparing well with the NBC poppy red applied to earlier Reliance/Weymann KFN 224 alongside. *John Bishop*

To replace the postwar Dennis Falcons, in 1967 East Kent took delivery of 10 Bedford VAS buses with Marshall bodywork. In this June 1973 view KJG 104E, on Ashford local service 507, is pursued through the town by a Maidstone & District AEC Reliance/Weymann, the latter with NBC insignia and corporate fleetnames applied to its traditional dark-green livery.

One of the final batch of AEC Reliance/Marshall buses delivered in 1968, OFN 727F, stands in Pencester Road, Dover, on 25 January 1975, the waiting passengers' overcoats confirming that the photograph was indeed taken in the depths of winter! Behind are a dual-purpose Reliance/Park Royal of 1960 and a Leyland Leopard/Marshall bus dating from 1963 but acquired from Southdown in 1971.
John Bishop

delivered in 1965 brought the single-deck service bus back into the fleet. These four vehicles (DJG 355-8C) were of particular interest in that their chassis were originally intended to be bodied as touring coaches and were thus to full coach specification, with the AH590 engine; in the event, they were given standard BET-style 51-seat bus bodies by Marshall. A further 10 51-seat buses (KJG 571-80E) followed in 1967, while 25 similar vehicles were delivered in 1968, but with 53 seats and based on the standard bus chassis; these had the larger AH691 engine and were registered OFN 708-32F.

By 1967 the normal-control Dennis Falcons were 17 years old and very outdated. Replacements came in the form of 10 Bedford VAS1s. The VAS was a successor to the popular Bedford OB of the 'Fifties, being a front-engined short-wheelbase chassis fitted with a Bedford 300 diesel engine and capable of taking bodywork with up to 30 seats. Unlike the OB it was of forward-control layout, with a full front and a narrow entrance behind the front wheels. East Kent's examples (KJG 104-13E) were fitted with 29-seat Marshall 'Cambrette' bodies to an angular design more often associated with the Bristol LH chassis. Later in life four of these little Bedfords would be converted into 'executive coaches', each being fitted with 18 seats taken from the Beadle-bodied AEC Reliance touring coaches.

In 1968 yet another make of body made its debut in the fleet, Willowbrook supplying the 49-seat coach bodies on eight AEC Reliance chassis (OJG 130-7F); these were basically standard BET bus bodies with side mouldings to match the Park Royal coaches. By this time, however, events were taking place nationally that would have far-reaching effects on the Company (as will become apparent in Chapter 8), and these coaches, together with the final batch of Reliance buses, would be the last vehicles delivered under the old regime.

7. AN INNOVATIONS CATALOGUE

Experiments, conversions and the Continental connection

With the return of the holidaymakers after the war the open-top double-decker had become a popular attraction at seaside resorts around the country. Usually the vehicles used were buses that were too old for front-line service but could still manage to trundle up and down a promenade for five or six months of the year, and in many places utility double-deckers were proving ideal for such work.

For a company whose area was bounded on three sides by the sea, East Kent was surprisingly slow at introducing open-toppers, and it was not until 1959 that it carried out its first conversions. Six utility Guys were chosen — BJG 339/53/4, Park Royal-bodied examples of 1944, and BJG 461/72/5, from the 1945 batch with highbridge Weymann bodywork. The modifications were fairly basic, involving the removal of the roof and upper-deck windows but leaving the lower quarter of the front windows as a windshield. The body sides were made higher as a safety measure. They were painted cream with cherry-red waistband and wings and were put to work on two new services on the Isle of Thanet. Over the years these services would be extended and eventually linked to form a 16-mile coastal service between Pegwell Bay and Minnis Bay.

Open-top conversion is a very handy remedy for buses that have met with a low bridge, as was the case with FFN 380, converted after just such an accident in 1962. Modifications were similar to those carried out on the utility Guys, but instead of building up the body sides, safety rails were fitted to the top deck. FFN 380 was put to work on a new service 45 operating between Herne Bay and Reculver. A further eight buses from the same batch, together with three Arabs from the GFN-registered batch, were similarly converted between 1968 and 1970, replacing the utilities and providing sufficient vehicles for a new service between Folkestone and Dover, which was to last for only a few years.

The final open-top conversions to fall within the scope of this book were effected in 1972/3 and involved seven of the full-front

Regents of 1959, which, due to service reductions, were sufficient to replace all of the Guys. On these the lower halves of the upper-deck windows were left *in situ*, as were the complete front windows.

In the late 'Fifties economic pressures were demanding that the more unremunerative services, particularly those in rural areas, be converted to OMO. At that time the 60 CFN-registered Dennis Lancet buses delivered in the 1947-9 period still had plenty of life left in them, but their half-cab, rear-entrance layout made them unsuitable for OMO. In 1956 the Company converted CFN 141 to front entrance and equipped it for one-man operation, but the result was not as successful as had been hoped, and in 1958 the vehicle was sent to Park Royal for a more comprehensive conversion to be carried out. As a result of this a further 25 Lancets were similarly treated, either by Park Royal or its

Park Royal FFN 378, its 'Round London Sightseeing Tour' advertisement indicative of a recent spell on loan to London Transport, while just visible on the right of the picture is none other than JG 9938, the prewar Leyland TS8 since beautifully restored to original condition.
John Bishop

associate, Charles Roe of Leeds.
As well as having the entrance
moved to the front, they were
given a completely new front end
featuring a fairly modern-looking
full front with a new grille (shaped
rather like a television screen!)
and a single-line destination
screen mounted in the front dome.
The front bulkhead was removed,
and the engine compartment
covered in a thick blanket of glass
wool to deaden the noise. The cab
floor was lowered by about a foot
to bring it into line with the
saloon, and this involved
shortening the steering column
and making similar adjustments to
brake, accelerator and clutch
pedals, as well as the hand brake.
To facilitate a lower windscreen
level the radiator had also to be
shortened. The result was a practical vehicle, suitable for OMO,
that had a modern appearance, at least from the front. However,
it was a pity that, with such a thorough conversion, a little more
attention could not have been paid to the rest of the body. The
fitting of sliding vents and the removal of the metal louvres and
roof mouldings would have created an altogether more modern
appearance and prevented the vehicle from looking what it was
— an old bus with a new front. Nevertheless, these converted
Lancets put in sterling service, most being 20 years old when
eventually withdrawn.

Over the years East Kent, like most companies, had on loan a
number of demonstration vehicles, some of which resulted in
orders' being placed, some fading into obscurity. Among the
more obscure vehicles to grace the roads of east Kent were a
Willowbrook-bodied Foden double-decker, an underfloor-
engined Dennis Pelican single-decker (the only one ever
completed) and a Mercedes-Benz O302 coach. Perhaps one of
the most interesting was the appearance in service of London
Transport RMF1254 (254 CLT), which spent three months with
the Company in 1963. Apart from those operated on behalf of
BEA, this was London's sole forward-entrance Routemaster.

With its AEC chassis and 69-seat Park Royal body, it would have
fitted well into the East Kent fleet, but this was not to be, the only
operator outside London to take the type being Northern General
— a pity, for the Routemaster would have looked quite superb in
East Kent colours, as indeed it did in Northern's similar livery.

Despite being known as the 'Garden of England', the eastern
part of Kent frequently suffers severe weather, partly because of
its proximity to the North Sea, and disruption of bus services due
to heavy snowfalls has been a regular hazard. The winter of 1940
was particularly bad — as if the Company hadn't enough on its
plate already, with troops arriving from the Commonwealth
countries. The winter of early 1947 was the coldest on record,
and snow covered most of the East Kent area from mid-January
until mid-March. The winter of 1962/3 was also memorable,
with heavy snow that fell at Christmas and lasted for weeks.
Even at sunny Eastbourne, it was reported, the sea was frozen for
100ft from the shore; some drifts in east Kent were almost as
high as a double-decker, and in one instance a Dennis Falcon had
to be rescued from 8ft of snow.

Floods have been another recurring problem. On the night of
31 January 1953 a combination of gales and high tides caused

flooding on the East Coast from Yorkshire to Kent, and high seas cut the railway line in several places between London and the North Kent coast. East Kent staff were called out, and 30 coaches that had been delicensed for the winter were rapidly made ready and pressed into service, dispensation being received for them to operate without licences! Whatever the challenge, East Kent was able to meet it.

The proximity of the East Kent area to mainland Europe had already had devastating effects on the Company's fortunes during two world wars. But it also had its benefits.

It seemed that, whatever East Kent did, it did with caution. Whether it was the operation of double-deckers, underfloor-engined coaches or open-toppers, it deliberated long and hard before taking the plunge. Continental touring was no exception, and it was not until 1950 that the first East Kent vehicle set wheels on Continental soil. The vehicle concerned was EFN 587, a brand-new Dennis Lancet, which had had its seating capacity reduced for the occasion. The tour, to the South of France, proved a success, and over subsequent years the Continental Tours Programme was extended and expanded.

In 1953 East Kent linked with Europabus, an organisation operating express services on mainland Europe. This arrangement made it possible to travel from London to Dover by East Kent coach, then by ferry to Ostend and by Europabus coach to Frankfurt. After a slow start, the facility became popular, and a number of East Kent coaches appeared in the pale-blue Europabus livery.

As well as the sea ports, Lympne airport was also within the Company's territory, and this led to a similar contract with Skyways whereby passengers were conveyed from Victoria to Lympne by East Kent coach; they would then fly to Beauvais airport, before continuing thence by coach to Paris. East Kent vehicles employed on such work wore a special livery incorporating a pale-blue waistband with 'Skyways Coach-Air' lettering. The arrangement ceased following the collapse of Skyways in 1971.

A further adventurous step was taken in 1969, when East Kent began to use British Rail's Seaspeed hovercraft service for excursions to northern France. Since the 'Sixties the ports of Folkestone, Dover and Ramsgate have also been the source of much contract work, which has seen vehicles in a wide range of liveries operating services between rail and ferry or hovercraft terminals.

From 1969 East Kent was able to take advantage of British Rail's recently introduced Seaspeed Dover–Boulogne hovercraft service to run day tours to Northern France. Here Willowbrook-bodied AEC Reliance OJG 131F carefully negotiates the ramp of the SRN4 hovercraft *Princess Margaret*. *The Omnibus Society*

45

8. TWILIGHT

A change of ownership — and another of engine position

In 1968 BET sold its bus interests to the Government-owned Transport Holding Company, East Kent and the other BET subsidiaries becoming nationalised companies. This was followed on 1 January 1969 by the formation of the National Bus Company, into which all the former BET and THC companies (plus a few others) were absorbed. As is usual with such takeovers there was initially little outward sign of any change apart from the application of advertisements announcing that East Kent was 'proud to be a part of the National Bus Company', which was probably far from the truth.

On the vehicle front the first year or so under NBC control saw the fulfilment of orders placed before its creation, and any changes in policy were owed more to the dictates of the manufacturing industry than to those of NBC itself. Whilst Maidstone & District had been one of the very first users of the rear-engined double-decker, its neighbours, East Kent and Southdown, had stuck steadfastly to the front-engined chassis. However, by 1969 there was little choice, production of front-engined buses having all but ceased. Both companies, perhaps surprisingly, turned to the Daimler Fleetline for their double-deck requirements, Southdown specifying bodies by its normal supplier, Northern Counties, and East Kent doing likewise by ordering 72-seat bodywork by Park Royal.

The early rear-engined double-deckers were generally agreed to be unattractive box-like vehicles, with single-skin domes and windows which differed in depth between upper and lower decks — all reminiscent of MCW's lightweight Orion body and not dissimilar to East Kent's half-cab Regent Vs. However, by 1969, when East Kent received its Fleetlines, bodywork of rear-engined 'deckers was into its second generation, and the Park Royal bodywork fitted was a worthy successor to some of the classics that had gone before. With large side windows, of equal depth on both decks, and slightly V-shaped windscreens, it was amongst the most attractive rear-engined double-deckers built, certainly at that time, and in East Kent's beautiful cherry red and ivory looked magnificent. The design was later used as the basis for bodywork supplied on Atlantean chassis to a number of NBC companies, notably London Country, Ribble and Southdown, but these had a fussy curved top to the windscreen that detracted from the clean lines of the East Kent version. Registered RFN 953-72G, the Fleetlines were soon sent to Thanet, where they were used as OMO vehicles.

By the late 'Sixties the rear-engine layout was very much in vogue for saloons as well as for double-deckers, and all the major chassis manufacturers were offering rear-engined chassis, which met with varying degrees of success. Not surprisingly, East Kent opted for the AEC Swift — a model that, under the name of 'Merlin', was entering service in large numbers with London Transport. East Kent initially took 10 (RJG 200-9G), delivered in 1969 with 51-seat bodywork by Marshall. Because of the lower floor at the front of this type of chassis, many bodybuilders employed a stepped waistline, with shallower windows at the rear, but Marshall used a straight waistline, so that at first glance these buses appeared little different from the Reliances that had gone before. A further 15 similar vehicles (VJG 185-99J) were delivered in 1970/1.

The year 1970 also saw a large intake of coaches, all on AEC Reliance 691 chassis. Eight (UFN 480-7H), for tour work, had 40-seat Duple Commander IV bodywork. The remainder (VFN 35-40H and VJG 474-9J) marked a departure for East Kent inasmuch as they had Plaxton Panorama Elite bodies, of varying seating capacities. Four (476-9) were delivered in Skyways livery, one of these (477) being fitted with second-hand aircraft seats for display at an air show in Amsterdam; however, none entered service as such, and all received standard livery following the collapse of Skyways. The VJG batch were also noteworthy in being East Kent's first 12m vehicles; they would be joined the following year by a quartet of similar 53-seat coaches (WJG 470-3J) and 14 11m 49-seaters (WJG 138-51J).

It had been a long time since any second-hand vehicles had

been purchased, but in 1971, to speed up the introduction of OMO in the Folkestone area, no fewer than 30 Marshall-bodied Leyland Leopards were acquired from Southdown. These consisted of Southdown's entire 1963 batch of 25 buses (265-89 AUF) and five from the following year's intake (100-4 CUF). The AUF batch had traditional curved rear domes, while the CUFs had the later BET-standard peaked domes and wrap-around rear windows. All were instantly recognisable by the traditional Southdown V-shaped moulding on the front panel.

At the end of 1971 came 12 AEC Swifts that introduced Alexander bodywork to the fleet. Registered YJG 581-92K they were to Alexander's 'W'-type design and were of seven-bay construction, resulting in narrow windows, the front four of which were deeper, with waistline stepped up towards the rear. Of additional interest is that these vehicles (and to some extent the ex-Southdown Leopards) replaced an order for 15 Alexander-bodied Daimler Fleetlines, the chassis of which were fitted with Eastern Coach Works bodywork and delivered to Southdown as its 385-99 (XUF 385-99K). The Alexander-bodied Swifts were also noteworthy in being the last vehicles to be delivered in traditional East Kent livery.

From then on it was all downhill. In the eyes of the National Bus Company big was beautiful, and companies were merged to form larger units: Thames Valley and Aldershot & District combined to become Alder Valley, Wilts & Dorset was absorbed into Hants & Dorset, and Southdown took over Brighton, Hove & District. Maidstone & District and East Kent never actually merged, retaining their individual liveries and fleetnames, but management was shared, and when a fleet-numbering system was eventually introduced, in 1977, this was designed to fit in with M&D's existing scheme.

East Kent's first rear-engined double-deckers, delivered in the spring and early summer of 1969, were 20 Daimler Fleetlines with handsome Park Royal bodywork. They were allocated to Thanet for OMO work and would always be associated with that garage; still looking immaculate when photographed in July 1974, RFN 958G is seen on Margate–Broadstairs–Ramsgate route 64. *John Bishop*

East Kent's first rear-engined vehicles arrived in 1969 in the shape of 10 Marshall-bodied AEC Swifts, these buses representing a departure from the Reliance model which had served the Company so well. One of this first batch, RJG 202G, stands on layover in Canterbury bus station on a hot June day in 1973. Although still in traditional colours it claims to be 'proud to be part of the National Bus Company'! *John Bishop*

Buses began to appear in the NBC corporate livery of poppy red with a white band, which didn't look too bad when freshly applied but soon faded to a matt pinky-orange. Coaches received a 'livery' of all-over white that did nothing for their appearance and confused the travelling public, who could no longer distinguish one company's coaches from another's. All in all it was a time best forgotten, so let us end our story here with images of those full-front Regent Vs, Leyland Tigers speeding from London to the Kent Coast and, of course, those magnificent Guy Arabs, for those truly were the 'Glory Days'.

But what about the East Kent bus, mentioned in the Introduction, that co-starred with Brigitte Bardot? That was JG 8207, a 1936 Leyland TD4 that had been rebodied by Park Royal in 1949 and appeared in the 1959 film *Babette Goes to War*. Set in 1940, the film tells the story of a young French girl who escapes from France and arrives in Kent; with some lively female companions she then sets off on a bus trip to London, which is where JG 8207 comes in. For the purposes of the film the bus, then still in East Kent ownership, was given wartime livery, masked headlights and white blackout markings. If you've seen the film, whether you watched Brigitte Bardot or the TD4 might indicate how much of an East Kent fan you are. Your authors drooled over both!

▲ A development unthinkable prior to the formation of NBC was the acquisition of second-hand vehicles, but in 1971 no fewer than 30 Leyland Leopard buses (themselves a departure for East Kent, albeit fitted with Marshall bodywork of a style already fitted to the Company's AEC Reliances) were transferred from Southdown. Seen in Hythe in June 1973, 267 AUF was already eight years old when acquired and would be withdrawn in 1975, the remainder following by the end of 1977. *John Bishop*

The final delivery of Swifts to East Kent, late in 1971, comprised a batch of 12 fitted with Alexander's stylish W-type bodywork. They would always be associated with the Dover area, where YJG 589K is seen on local route 301 in June 1973. *John Bishop*

▶

Retained by East Kent as an office, JG 9938 fortunately lasted long enough for its historic importance to be realised. A Leyland Tiger TS8 new in 1938 with 32-seat Park Royal coachwork, it is seen promoting the 'Freedom Ticket' at Hastings coach station in September 1976; this was during the NBC era, when resources were shared with Maidstone & District. The cricket ground and surrounding area have since been redeveloped as a large retail complex.
John Bishop

Canterbury bus station on a busy day in the early 1960s is the setting for CFN 112, a 35-seat Park Royal-bodied Dennis Lancet of 1949. Sixty such Lancets were delivered 1947-9 with CFN registrations, a further 12 having CJG registrations. Examples of both batches would be extensively rebuilt for pay-as-you-enter (PAYE) service, thus extending their lives, but CFN 112 would not be among them, being withdrawn in 1963 still in broadly original condition. *Howard Butler*

In 1958/9 26 of the Dennis Lancet III/Park Royal buses were extensively rebuilt with forward entrance and modernised full front, thereby losing the distinctive Dennis radiator, CFN 165 being seen on layover in Court Street, Faversham, in the mid-1960s. At this time an extensive rural network was still operated, service 31 (Faversham–Chilham) running only on Friday, Saturday and Sunday. *Howard Butler*

Deal bus station always provided splendid opportunities for nearside views such as this shot of lowbridge all-Leyland Titan PD1 CJG 939 of 1947. When this photograph was taken in 1965 this bus had only a year of service left but despite its 18 years was still employed on the main-road route 60 to Margate. In the immediate postwar period many BET companies took delivery of the Leyland Titan PD1s with painted radiator shells; in most cases these were eventually chromed or cleaned of paint, but on East Kent's batch they remained red. Also of note is the bus's advertisement, whereby the more Kensitas cigarettes you smoked the more gifts you could obtain! *John Bishop*

A brace of Park Royal-bodied Guy Arabs bathe in the sunshine in April 1967, only the reduced destination display marring the impression of 'glory days'. Leading Guy EFN 209 advertises the Hoverlloyd service from Ramsgate to Calais, which greatly reduced the time needed to cross the English Channel. On dry land, service 52 had a six-minute headway between Ramsgate and Margate, although neither vehicle here appears to be in any hurry — perhaps the Harbour Café holds a clue as to the whereabouts of the crews! *Howard Butler*

Deal was served by a number of local and town routes, and in 1965, when
this photograph was taken, these were still crew-operated. Lowbridge
Park Royal-bodied Guy Arab EFN 177 dating from 1950 leads one of the
highbridge (FFN-registered) batch of 1951, both vehicles displaying full-
size destination blinds incorporating 'via' points. Note also that, unlike
many other operators, East Kent resisted the temptation to paint the
wheel-hub rings on its vehicles. *John Bishop*

Any visitor to Canterbury bus station (to the east of the city centre) would be confronted by a varied assortment of East Kent buses waiting to take up duty. Prominent in this view is lowbridge Park Royal-bodied Guy Arab III EFN 179 of 1950, whilst behind can be seen a Dennis Lancet UF coach and three AEC Regent Vs. The advertisement for Ben Truman Ale reminds us that in the mid-1960s, when this photograph was taken, brewing was a major industry in Kent. *Howard Butler*

The picturesque town of Rye in East Sussex had a network of routes operated by East Kent to Camber, Lydd, Ashford and Hastings. Lowbridge Park Royal-bodied Guy Arab III EFN 172 and a smart but unidentified AEC Reliance/Weymann are seen in the mid-1960s in the station approach, where during the summer months there would always be at least a couple of vehicles waiting to be photographed. *Howard Butler*

Canterbury bus station has always been a superb location for photography, even on a hot summer Sunday in 1965, when this view was recorded. A 1949-built Dennis Falcon with 20-seat Dennis bodywork, EFN 557 was one of a batch of 15 delivered for more lightly trafficked routes such as the 20 to Waltham. *John Bishop*

A trip around the parking area adjacent to Dover garage would nearly always yield a coach or two, and on this occasion the rewards were rich, comprising two Dennis Lancet IIIs with 32-seat Park Royal coachwork. Dating from 1950, EFN 594/5 bask in the summer of 1965 next to an underfloor-engined Lancet UF/Duple. Redevelopment has since robbed enthusiasts of this photographic location. *John Bishop*

Canterbury is steeped in history and was once surrounded by a wall with entrances at strategic positions, the surviving West Gate featuring in this view of highbridge Park Royal-bodied Guy Arab III FFN 379 on local route 27A. The senior citizen with his cloth cap looks at peace with himself as he endeavours to light his pipe. *Howard Butler*

The 8ft width of the Park Royal bodywork (wth a hint of London Transport RT class) is shown to good effect in this view of Guy Arab III FFN 384 and serves to emphasise the type's characteristic narrow radiator. Canterbury city service 28 was tolerated only at the rear entrance of the hospital, it seems! Also worthy of comment is the street furniture; the 'NO WAITING' signs seem peculiarly British, while the concept of *free* parking is today almost unheard of in urban areas, where parking space of any kind is constantly at a premium. *Howard Butler*

In the 1960s a number of the 1951 batch of Guy Arab IIIs were converted to open-top format for service in the Isle of Thanet. Even when this use came to an end they continued to give useful service, as demonstrated by FFN 375, engaged in driver-training work at Westwood (Thanet) garage in July 1973. Athough now downgraded, it still manages to look immaculate, such was the sense of pride in the fleet felt by employees. *John Bishop*

East Kent, ever faithful to Park Royal, chose the company to body its first batch of Leyland Royal Tigers. How superb they looked, their ornate coachwork livery enhanced by stainless-steel strips and a livery of two-tone red and cream. By the time FFN 448 was photographed in July 1965 this grand vehicle dating from 1951 had been demoted from front-line touring to private hire. The location is the Sandgate Police Training School near Folkestone, where the photographer was supposed to be training as a police officer for Sussex Police, but clearly the coach was the star attraction! *John Bishop*

Seen basking in brilliant sunshine in the mid-1960s is 1954 Dennis
Lancet UF coach HJG 19, its underfloor-engined chassis layout and the
smooth lines of its Duple Ambassador bodywork representing a quantum
leap when compared with the Dennis vehicles of just four years earlier.
The Vauxhall Victor Model F in the background would make for an
interesting classic car today, in view of corrosion problems commonplace
in the 1960s. Note also the use of an old wheel as the base of a sign.
Howard Butler

In the early 1950s a number of
BET companies took delivery
of Beadle chassisless coaches
to ease vehicle shortages and
make economic use of prewar
AEC and Leyland running
units which in themselves
were perfectly sound.
East Kent was no exception
and used Leyland Titan TD5
chassis from the AJG batch.
This offside view of GFN 280
— numerically the last of 28
such vehicles — was recorded
at Margate in the summer of
1965. The Hillman Minx
convertible behind is worthy
of note, being comparatively
rare even then. *John Bishop*

Beadle-Leyland rebuild GFN 263 basks in the sun at London's Victoria Coach Station in the mid-1960s, its East Kent livery shining brightly in the best traditions of this operator. In the background are another East Kent vehicle, in the shape of a Park Royal-bodied AEC Reliance, and a Black & White Motorways Reliance/Duple. Film buffs may wish to note that *Cleopatra* was showing at the Dominion and *Tom Jones* at the London Pavilion; while these can still be enjoyed, GFN 263 alas cannot. *Howard Butler*

In 1953 East Kent took delivery of 30 Park Royal-bodied Guy Arab IVs with New Look fronts in lieu of the original distinctive radiator, which modification must have hindered maintenance. Seen in the mid-1960s when over 10 years old, GFN 914 still looks pristine as it waits to depart Folkestone bus station on the hourly service to Canterbury. *Howard Butler*

Two of the 1957 delivery of Park Royal-bodied Guy Arab IVs are seen in this early spring view in Pencester Road, Dover in the mid-1960s. With an eager schoolboy in pride of place at the front of the upper deck, MFN 902 prepares to depart on 'main road' route 87 to Ramsgate. *Howard Butler*

Three years separated delivery of the GFN- and MFN-registered Guy Arab IVs. Unless compared side by side they appeared similar, but close inspection revealed the latter batch to be much more upright in frontal profile, as apparent in this view of MFN 884 and GFN 934 framed by the awning of Folkestone bus station in the summer of 1965. *John Bishop*

An almost timeless scene, actually recorded in May 1973, as dual-purpose AEC Reliance/Weymann KFN 217 bound for Hastings passes sister vehicle KFN 236 on layover in the Station Approach at Rye, East Sussex. East Kent's routes in the Hastings and Rye areas would shortly be 'rationalised' and passed to neighbouring Maidstone & District, the traditional red East Kent bus stops giving way to standard items and the Reliances being transferred eastwards. *John Bishop*

A 1956 AEC Reliance with dual-purpose Weymann body, LJG 324 heads west out of Folkestone town centre on route 100 to Golden Valley Estate in May 1973. Seen heading towards Folkestone, beyond the Morris Marina, is an ex-Southdown Leyland Leopard/Marshall. The lack of traffic and parked cars makes for a tranquil scene. Time was when all traffic travelled via the town centre, but nowadays ring roads and traffic management take one speedily onwards to Dover on the left. *John Bishop*

It is a matter of some regret that Beadle should have ceased its bodybuilding activities at a time when it was producing some of its most elegant and well-proportioned designs, exemplified by AEC Reliance MJG 46 of 1957, photographed deep in Eastern National territory at Basildon, Essex, in the company of a Bristol K double-decker and a Bristol LS coach.
Howard Butler

An AEC Reliance with Beadle bodywork of rather bland design (considering this was a dual-purpose vehicle), NFN 343 is seen outside Folkestone bus station (out of shot to our right) in May 1973, by which time it was some 16 years old, having been delivered in 1957.

The practice of using an old wheel as the base for a temporary bus stop is again evident. The building site behind would eventually become the headquarters of Saga. *John Bishop*

In 1958/9, when operators such as neighbouring Maidstone & District were purchasing rear-engined Leyland Atlanteans, East Kent turned to the AEC Regent V to satisfy its double-deck requirements. This marked a departure from the previous patronage of Guy Motors, which supplier had served the Company well, but fell into line with the single-deck fleet. Bodywork was still by Park Royal, albeit now with forward entrance. The initial batch of 40, with full front, is represented by PFN 868 at Margate in the mid-1960s. This batch soon became known affectionately as the 'Puffins' and would give superb service to the Company, many remaining in normal service until the mid-1970s.
Howard Butler

The flared trousers of the girl with the pushchair date this picture to the early 1970s, when seven AEC Regent Vs of the initial, 1959 batch were converted to open-top to replace Guy Arabs. The first, PFN 853, was so treated in July 1972 and is seen shortly afterwards at Minis Bay, Birchington, about to depart on the long coastal route 69 to Ramsgate, taking in all the sights the Isle of Thanet has to offer. *John Bishop*

Still fitted with coach seating, 1960 AEC Reliance/Park Royal TFN 433 had nearly two more years of valuable service to give when photographed on the forecourt of Westwood (Thanet) garage on 15 August 1975 — well into the NBC era. The state of the destination screen and the grey wheels are no match for past glories, but somehow the quality still shines through. *John Bishop*

In 1971 some of the AEC Reliance/Park Royal dual-purpose vehicles were adapted for Seaspeed work by the fitting of luggage pens and were painted in BR Rail blue and white. Here, in June 1974, TFN 411 awaits passengers at Dover Priory station before departing for the port as similar TFN 418, still in full East Kent livery, fills with luggage. *John Bishop*

In 1960 East Kent took delivery of TJG 440, a Harrington Crusader-bodied
Ford Thames. Although possibly an odd choice for a fleet dominated by
AEC and Dennis chassis, it nevertheless gave 11 years of faithful service.
This mid-1960s photograph, taken at Farthing Corner service station in
Gillingham, depicts a livery variation popular with enthusiasts and public
alike. On the left of the picture is immaculate Beadle-bodied AEC Reliance
MJG 44 of 1957 on a new express service (X34) to Clacton via the then-
new Dartford Tunnel. *Howard Butler*

One of a batch of 18 dual-purpose Park Royal-bodied AEC Reliances delivered in 1961, WFN 504 was 12 years old by the time this photograph was taken in Deal bus station in July 1973 but still looked resplendent in traditional East Kent red and cream. Route 78 ran to Shepherdswell via Eythorne — places synonymous with the East Kent Light Railway and the erstwhile coal-mining industry. *John Bishop*

In 1962 the Company purchased three low-height AEC Bridgemaster/Park Royal vehicles for use on Dover town service 129, which passed under a low bridge. Appealing to a fairly limited market, the Bridgemaster would never be as popular nationally as the Regent V, but East Kent's trio gave good service on their intended route, as demonstrated by YJG 807 in the early 1960s. Note the Skyways advertisement (illuminated at night) promoting travel to Paris by coach/air for £8.
Howard Butler

In 1961 East Kent took into stock the first 16 of many AEC Regent Vs with a revised style of Park Royal bodywork, which some devotees of that coachbuilder felt were not as well-proportioned as its earlier products. Seen heading along the seafront at Margate on local route 49 in August 1975, WFN 834 demonstrates that the Company still provided full and informative destination displays, in contrast to many operators, which by this time had reduced their information.
John Bishop

Pictured standing in Canterbury bus station under a cloudless sky
in June 1973 is 1963 AEC Reliance/ Park Royal coach 6547 FN.
On the left is 1962 Reliance 531 FN, newly rebodied by Plaxton
— a fate which would befall 6547 FN the following year.
Only the corporate fleetname on dual-purpose Weymann-bodied
Reliance KFN 228 in the background gives hint of NBC influence.
John Bishop

A photograph taken at Dover in June 1965, showing how varied was East Kent's coaching fleet — and how immaculate its condition — in the glory days.
Here we have 'four for the price of one'; from left to right are TFN 435, a dual-purpose Park Royal-bodied AEC Reliance of 1960, 526 FN (in Europabus blue) and 6539 FN, Park Royal-bodied Reliances new in 1962/3 respectively, and HJG 6, a 1954 Dennis Lancet UF with Duple Ambassador coachwork.
Both 526 FN and 6539 FN would be rebodied by Plaxton in the 1970s.
John Bishop

In the right conditions the yard beside the ex-Maidstone & District garage at Ashford would afford a splendid offside view. Present in July 1973 were AEC Regent V/ Park Royal AFN 770B — one of a batch of 20 delivered in 1964 and among the first East Kent vehicles with year-suffix registrations — and a number of dual-purpose Weymann-bodied Reliances, WFN 507 and an unidentified 'LJG' in differing styles of NBC poppy red and white comparing unfavourably with traditionally liveried KFN 233. *John Bishop*

A fascinating scene recorded in the early spring of 1966, with almost new Park Royal-bodied AEC Regent V GJG 734D passing the then Maidstone & District garage in Ashford on local route 125. A coach-liveried 'WFN' Reliance stands in the yard of the adjacent East Kent garage. In the foreground a mother negotiates her coach-built pram up the kerb while looking anxiously at her child further on. To the left an old British motorcycle with sidecar waits to pull out safely. *Howard Butler*

Photographed at Canterbury when almost brand-new, AFN 498B, a 1964 AEC Reliance with 34-seat Duple Commander coachwork, prepares to depart on a tour to the Peak District and the English Lakes. Just visible behind the coach are a Maidstone & District double-decker on route 67 to Maidstone and a Weymann bus-bodied Reliance. Parked in the background are a Guy Arab/Park Royal and a 1957 AEC Reliance/Beadle DP. *Howard Butler*

The conductor, in grey summer uniform with red lapels, seems to be in jolly mood as Park Royal-bodied Reliance DJG 609C prepares to pull away from Canterbury bus station in July 1973. On the left dual-purpose Reliance KFN 228 again manages to squeeze in on the act, while in the background is an example of what had become East Kent's standard double-decker, the AEC Regent V/Park Royal, in this case one of the 1963 delivery. *John Bishop*

At Deal, in the vicinity of the bus station, it was the accepted practice to
board a bus in the road, as apparent from this scene recorded in July 1974.
Route 13 would take the main road north to the picturesque town of
Sandwich before continuing inland into Canterbury. AEC Reliance
DJG 355C, with standard BET Federation Marshall bodywork of a style
common to most BET companies, was one of a quartet delivered in 1965
that had been intended to receive coach bodywork. Behind is AEC Swift
VJG 189J with similar Marshall bodywork. *John Bishop*

In May 1974 construction work in the environs of Folkestone bus station seemed endless, but Marshall-bodied AEC Reliance OFN 727F is apparently oblivious as it departs on route 90 to Dover, which will take it via the main trunk road over the steep hills out of Folkestone — a task to which this type of vehicle was more than equal. The two elderly ladies by the poppy-red AEC Regent V look apprehensive as the Reliance takes its leave! *John Bishop*

When the Dennis Falcons
of 1949/50 fell due for
replacement East Kent chose
the Bedford VAS1, with
29-seat bodywork by Marshall
of Cambridge. Almost brand-
new when photographed in
the spring of 1967, KJG 108E
was one of a batch of 10 such
vehicles, used on lightly
trafficked routes including the
92 from Dover to Capel (or, to
quote the East Kent timetable,
'Capel Street Shelter').
Although the main road is
visible in the background, the
92 would serve more rural
areas before returning to
Dover. *Howard Butler*

Close scrutiny of the same
vehicle photographed in July
1974 reveals that it has now
been converted to 'executive
coach' specification using
18 seats from the 1957 (MJG)
batch of AEC Reliance/
Beadle touring coaches.
The application of red/white/
grey coach livery, together
with additional trim and wheel
embellishers, transforms its
appearance as it awaits its
driver on Deal seafront, but
the newly delivered Plaxton-
bodied Volvo B58 of Park's
of Hamilton nevertheless
provides a marked contrast.
John Bishop

In 1969, with the AEC Regent no longer available, East Kent adopted the rear-engined layout by now *de rigueur* for double-deckers. The chassis chosen was the Daimler Fleetline, fitted with well-proportioned Park Royal bodywork. The batch of 20 would prove to be the Company's last new double-deckers until well into the NBC era, such that they were still the newest in the fleet when RFN 958G was photographed in July 1974. Seen in Ramsgate on route 64, it shows how the superb East Kent livery enhanced these already handsome buses; note also once again the retention of a full destination display. The wall of the three-storey building cannot hide the outline of a neighbouring structure that has been demolished, possibly as a result of wartime bomb damage. *John Bishop*

As East Kent entered the 1970s its buying policy was 100% AEC, as exemplified by VFN 39H, an AEC Reliance with Plaxton Panorama Elite coachwork, delivered in 1970. This view was taken in Folkestone bus station in May 1973, NBC influence by now being apparent in the form of a poppy-red AEC Regent V. Discernible on the building behind is the distinctive scroll of Martin Walker, which coachbuilder (long since defunct) was noted for its caravanette conversions of small van-type vehicles, including the Bedford CF. *John Bishop*

One of East Kent's first batch of 12m vehicles, AEC Reliance VJG 476J,
with Plaxton Panorama Elite coachwork, is seen at Canterbury bus station
in June 1973. Delivered in November 1970 in Skyways livery, this vehicle
saw various changes to its seating arrangements but, following the demise
of Skyways, was reseated to 53 by Midland Red and repainted into East Kent
livery, its entry into service thus being delayed until mid-1971.
The size of the East Kent fleetname is such that the vehicle seems
embarrassed to bear it! *John Bishop*

The Marshall bodywork on VJG 191J, pictured outside Deal bus station in July 1973, disguises the fact that this is not an AEC Reliance but an example of the rear-engined Swift model. This bus was one of the Company's second batch of Swifts, the first having been delivered in 1969. Three years old when this view was recorded, VJG 191J had lost its newness but still looked smart in East Kent's superb livery of red and cream.
John Bishop

The third and final batch of AEC Swifts comprised 12 buses delivered late in 1971 and marked a departure in being bodied by Alexander, with that firm's stylish W-type bodywork.

They also turned out to be the last new vehicles delivered in East Kent's traditional red and cream. Although somewhat coach-like in appearance they always had bus seating and were used on local routes in Dover, where YJG 591K is pictured in August 1973, having been in service for nearly two years.

John Bishop

By 1971, when East Kent's final AEC Swifts were delivered, the National Bus Company was redeploying vehicles far and wide throughout the 'empire'. One such transfer saw the introduction of a chassis type new to East Kent — the Leyland Leopard — although the bodywork, by Marshall of Cambridge, was broadly similar in style to that on AEC Reliance buses new to the Company. Thirty in number, the Leopards in question came from Southdown Motor Services and are represented here by 280 AUF (formerly Southdown 680), seen approaching Folkestone bus station in May 1973. *John Bishop*

Acquired from Southdown (676) in 1971, Leyland Leopard/Marshall 276 AUF still looks resplendent in red and cream as it leaves Folkestone bus station on local route 103 in May 1973. The scene illustrates the continuing variety to be found in the East Kent fleet; visible in the background are two dual-purpose Weymann-bodied AEC Reliances, a Plaxton-bodied Reliance coach and, partly obscured by the ex-Southdown Leopard, a poppy-red Regent V. *John Bishop*

A rear nearside view of Leopard 278 AUF (ex-Southdown 678) in Folkestone bus station in May 1973, showing the more curved rear profile of the Marshall bodywork carried by most of these buses. As yet the influence of National Bus Company corporate identity on East Kent appears minimal, judging from the livery of the buses and the presence of traditional-style destination boards, but the Maidstone & District Leyland Atlantean in the background has already succumbed to NBC leaf green. *John Bishop*

A visit to Ashford garage in July 1974 would have yielded rich rewards for AEC enthusiasts, in the form of three Reliances built between 1957 and 1962. Although now 17 years old, MJG 45 still looks immaculate, while 521 FN, rebodied by Plaxton in 1972, sports old-style fleetnames (compare with 534 FN shown opposite). Visible on the right, meanwhile, is the rear of dual-purpose Park Royal-bodied example TFN 436, dating from 1960. *John Bishop*

The Station Approach at Rye, East Sussex, is thronged with holidaymakers in August 1974 as the inspector confers with the driver of 1962 AEC Reliance 534 FN, rebodied by Plaxton the previous year. NBC influence is apparent in the style of fleetname, but the application of a non-standard livery incorporating dark-red waistband and grey lower panels represents an act of defiance by East Kent. *John Bishop*

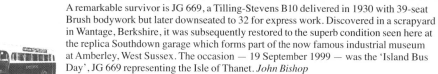

A remarkable survivor is JG 669, a Tilling-Stevens B10 delivered in 1930 with 39-seat Brush bodywork but later downseated to 32 for express work. Discovered in a scrapyard in Wantage, Berkshire, it was subsequently restored to the superb condition seen here at the replica Southdown garage which forms part of the now famous industrial museum at Amberley, West Sussex. The occasion — 19 September 1999 — was the 'Island Bus Day', JG 669 representing the Isle of Thanet. *John Bishop*